Martina Flor
THE BIG LEAP

Published by
Princeton Architectural Press
202 Warren Street
Hudson, New York 12534
www.papress.com

©2020 Martina Flor
First published in Spanish under the title *El Gran Salto*
   by Editorial Gustavo Gili
All rights reserved
Printed and bound in China
23 22 21 20 4 3 2 1 First edition

ISBN 978-1-61689-956-1

No part of this book may be used or reproduced in any manner without written permission from the publisher, except in the context of reviews.

Every reasonable attempt has been made to identify owners of copyright. Errors or omissions will be corrected in subsequent editions.

For Princeton Architectural Press:
Project editor: Parker Menzimer

For Studio Martina Flor:
Design: Martina Flor
Direction: Martina Flor
Layout: Elías Prado
Cover design: Elías Prado and Martina Flor
Photography: Soraya Cremallé Sa
Project management: Josefina Anglada

Library of Congress Cataloging-in-Publication data available upon request.

Martina Flor

THE BIG LEAP

A GUIDE TO FREELANCING FOR CREATIVES

Princeton Architectural Press · New York

CONTENTS

06 — **Introduction**

Chapter 1: On Freelancing

10 — Freelancer = Entrepreneur
11 — Scope Map
12 — Being Your Own Boss
15 — The Challenges of Freelancing
24 — Ease In or Just Leap?

Chapter 2: First Steps

30 — Your Professional Identity
30 — Presenting Your Work
35 — Building a Solid Portfolio and Being Your Own Client
39 — Introducing Yourself

Chapter 3: Generating Income

46 — Income Streams
46 — Client Commissions
48 — Trainings and Workshops
51 — Speaking Engagements
53 — Online Classes
56 — Creating and Selling Products
58 — Licensing Art and Design
61 — Other Opportunities

Chapter 4: Finding Clients

66 — Where and How to Find Clients
71 — Working with an Agent
76 — Building a Social Media Following

Chapter 5: Day-to-Day Administration

88 — Workspace
93 — Time Off
96 — Managing Your Finances
97 — Time Management
102 — Organizing Your Process

Chapter 6: Getting the Job Done, Part I—Securing the Assignment

108 — Receiving an Inquiry
110 — Types of Assignments
111 — Pricing Your Work
117 — Quotes and Estimates
120 — Sending a Quote
122 — Licensing

Chapter 7: Getting the Job Done, Part II—Executing the Assignment

128 — Executing the Assignment
128 — The Client Brief
130 — A Professional Work Process
139 — Getting Paid

Chapter 8: Sustainable Growth

146 — Keeping the Right Distance
146 — "Educating" Customers
147 — Working in Different Markets
148 — Defining Standards for Your Work
150 — Retaining Clients
151 — Attracting Better Assignments
153 — Taking Care of Your Most Important Tool: Yourself
156 — Dealing with the Competition

158 — **What's Next**
159 — **Afterword**
160 — **Acknowledgments**

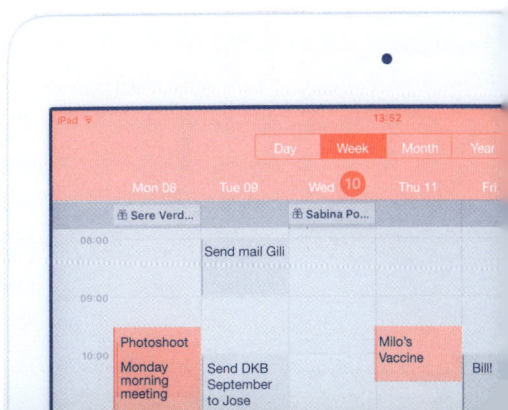

INTRODUCTION

Imagine a job that's tailor-made just for you. You set your own hours and do the work you love most. You choose when to work and when to take a vacation. You decide what color the walls of your office are, in which chair you are going to work, if your desk looks toward the window or faces the wall, and what brand of coffee you drink. This is a job you want to go to every day. It's your dream job. At the moment, that job doesn't exist. But there is someone who has the power to make it possible: you.

Of course, this will not happen overnight. But there are clear, practical steps you can take to make it happen. When you have your own business, you decide what kind of work you take on, and what kind of work you decline. There will no longer be a boss who will assign you projects. Actually, there will be, but that boss will be you.

The Motivation behind This Book

As creatives, we've spent a lot of time learning and mastering our craft and cultivating our talents, but usually not much time learning how to make a living with them! Many of us who went to art or design school left with no clue how to price our work, find clients, or run a business in the creative industry.

No wonder many of us give up on the idea of a dream job and instead get any old job anywhere! Thriving in business is an essential part of thriving in art, and I have good news for you: both are possible!

Teaching is a big part of my business, and it's a part I really enjoy. Through it, I encounter other creatives, illustrators, designers, architects, and calligraphers, and through that I've found answers to some of the more important questions you'll need to ask yourself when you are considering making the transition to becoming a freelancer: How do I price my work? How do I build my portfolio when I haven't yet had any clients? When and how do I take the big leap? How do I get an agent, and do I need one? I had the same questions when I started, and I would have loved to have a guide to show me the way.

And I'm not just talking about how to make a living and get by as a self-employed person. I'm talking about how to build a practice that you're truly proud of, that carries your mark and represents your vision, and that will ultimately make you happy.

This book may find you graduating from university, unsure of what you're going to do next. Maybe you're already a freelancer, but you're not doing the work you love or attracting the right clients. Maybe you're working in a company and are considering going freelance. To go freelance, you don't only need to know what it means to be self-employed, but also to understand the concrete steps to do so.

With *The Big Leap*, I've broken down the process of building a creative business into chunks, so that you can understand each step and approach your own process in a comprehensive, well-informed way. I offer everything I've learned on my own journey in the hopes that it will help you on yours.

I will explain the ins and outs of freelancing, including how to organize the most elementary aspects of your practice and build a sustainable independent business.

How to Use This Book

In this book I share many things that I learned in my experience setting up my own practice as a designer and lettering artist. Keep in mind that you are the one who will need to give everything you have during each step in this process, and my advice must be filtered through your own point of view. For this reason, I have reserved a sheet at the end of each chapter where you can make personal notes about some of the topics we will cover along the way. If you complete these end-of-chapter sheets, you will reach the end of the book with a road map that you can use to start your own creative business. I'm not going to lie to you: being a freelancer can be tough at times, but it's definitely an exciting adventure. Let's get ready to jump!

Martina Flor

1. On Freelancing

In this chapter, we look at what it means to be a freelancer: how to define the scope of your business, explore its benefits and challenges, and investigate the tools you need and may already have to get started.

Freelancer = Entrepreneur

As a freelancer, you are an entrepreneur. You will own this business, no matter its size and scope. You will decide on its direction, execute the work, search and connect with clients, invoice those clients, and pay the necessary bills for services that keep your business thriving. Sounds like a lot to do, doesn't it? It is, and that's why this may require a shift of attitude and perspective from you, the business owner.

In most cases, as an employee, one takes instructions from the boss. When there's work to be done, you execute that work. On days when there are no urgent deadlines, you might take the time to surf the internet, have an extra cup of coffee, or take a longer lunch than usual. When you're self-employed things are different: there is *always work to do*. Your daily work includes not only your creative work for clients, but many other aspects that you may not have had to deal with so far. When you're not doing client assignments, you are updating your website or portfolio with your most recent completed projects, paying an invoice from a subcontractor, or trying to engage the next client. To cover all your freelance bases, you will have to learn new things, such as how to manage your taxes as a self-employed person, how to run the software that maintains your website, and how to manage your time more efficiently.

Of course, in many cases, you will be able to work with collaborators. You can, for example, delegate your tax preparation to an accountant. You can hire a web designer to keep your online portfolio up-to-date. These are all possibilities and it is smart to make use of them, but even when you have help in certain areas, you will still be taking care of a lot more things than you have so far. Probably the biggest change you'll experience when going freelance: you'll be at the helm most of the time. Your stance and attitude must be active rather than passive. It all comes down to you.

Scope Map

The decision to become a freelancer is usually motivated by the desire to do work that you love, rather than work that is either unpleasant or "good enough." Because being self-employed involves so much responsibility, and can feel like more work than being employed by someone else, I suggest you compromise as little as possible and do work that keeps you happy and fulfilled—this will be your reward.

What you *can do* and what you *want to do* will help guide your freelance business. You might want to do illustration only, focus solely on photography, or make graphic design your meat and potatoes. And within your chosen field, you may want to focus on a specific area, such as culture, pharmaceuticals, or entertainment.

This is where a "scope map" comes in. At the end of this chapter, you'll find a worksheet for creating your own scope map. This map is a written document and not an actual map, and is made up of two things:

1. The things you can do:
This part of your map defines and clarifies the range of projects you can apply your skills to. For example, if you are a graphic designer, you can do corporate design, brochures, logos, layout, and editorial design, among many other things. If you're a photographer, you can photograph social events, art, and commercial products, or specialize in documentary images. Your skills are your resources that will define how you achieve your goals and grow your business.

2. The things you want to do:
This part of your map defines very precisely the job that you *want* to do. It's your true north, what's calling you, and where you envision yourself at your happiest.

When you first start out, you likely won't make enough to cover your expenses. The first work you take on will not necessarily align with the work you ultimately want to do. That's OK.
Do work at the start that will help you pay your bills while you spend time attracting more desirable commissions and projects. One thing to bear in mind: make sure those jobs you take to pay the bills do not prevent you from dedicating time to achieving your ultimate goals as a freelancer. Try to devote part of your day to projects that help you expand your portfolio in the direction you want to go. You can even try to complete those assignments that you don't like so much with the skills you want to use more often. For example, if you want to do more illustration, and you just took on an assignment for the design of a brochure, why not use your illustration skills to add some visual interest to the layout? Here the benefit is double: you pay the bills and expand your portfolio.

Keep your vison and goals in the forefront of your mind. Dedicating time to them is essential, as essential as having patience and giving your business time to develop. It isn't going to happen overnight. It will be a few months before you get into a rhythm and receive your first solid assignments—and those assignments will, ideally, bring in new assignments. This process will require your patience and perseverance, and a proactive attitude.

Being Your Own Boss

As a freelancer, you are the one who makes the decisions about all aspects of your business. This will allow you to mold your work life in whatever manner you wish—a truly fabulous prospect! Your personality and your way of life will have a direct impact on what you do. If you are an anxious person, it will affect your business in both helpful and challenging ways, as will being a slower person. If you work better at night than during the day, you can accommodate your own rhythms, by working with customers who are in another time zone, for example.

If you like to travel, you can apply to give talks at conferences or teach workshops in places you'd like to explore.

In this new venture of yours, you are the central point of everything you build. You will see how rewarding it can be to build something that is entirely your own.

The Potential to Earn More

Another piece of good news! Contrary to what many believe, a freelancer can have a substantially higher income than an employee. A freelancer can also earn the same as an employee but work considerably fewer hours. One assignment can help you pay for three months of living expenses, but only require one month of work. Depending on what you do, there are jobs that will earn you royalties, providing you with profit over time without you even having to work for it!

Your possible sources of income increase exponentially when you are self-employed because you can take advantage of your diverse range of skills. If, for example, you work with photography and love to teach, you can do work for clients, sell your photos, and teach classes and workshops. Later in this book we will discuss how to broaden the range of possibilities and how to price your work—one of the most important and complex aspects of your practice—and manage expenses in ways that increase your potential to generate more income.

Managing Your Schedule

Managing your schedule gives you great freedom to be flexible and independent, without having to ask anyone's permission to do anything. That said, you'll be doing work for clients, so you'll have to be available during certain time ranges so that you can conference when necessary.

Managing your own schedule will require a certain amount of self-discipline on your part. With no almighty boss dictating what must be done, following a schedule will require commitment.

Ideally, your workday should be tailored to you. If you like sleep, plan a workday that begins a little later than usual and stretches into the evening. You can also take Fridays off or work a half day when you want to. Forget about the structures you've followed up to now—your workdays can be any way you want! The important thing is that you carve out work hours for yourself and stick to them, so that your practice maintains orderand consistency.

Decision-Making

You will now be making decisions in all aspects of your working life: you will decide which commissions you decline and which you take, how much you charge, the best way to execute assignments. As I mentioned earlier, you'll choose your clients, and you'll stop working for those you don't like to work for. You will decide whether the walls of your workspace are green or yellow, if the office coffee is regular or hazelnut, and if you can take Monday morning off to go to the doctor or visit an old friend. You'll own this business in every way.

All the decisions you make are important, because they reflect your values, your priorities, and your personal brand. Your decisions will have the power to affect the progress of your practice. Don't fear doing things differently from how other freelancers are doing them. The only formula you must apply to make your business work is…your own.

Creating Your Personal Brand

Your logotype, the color on your letterhead, the design of your website, and even the way your dress and behave, are some of the things that define your personal brand.

Since you are a freelancer, you are your business; thus, your professional brand is also defined by who you are: how you present yourself when interacting with clients, including your style of dress, your hairstyle, and your overall demeanor, including the way you speak to customers and whether or not you smile when you are introduced to a colleague. You are your personal brand.

From now on, each of your assignments will say something about how you approach a project, and, based on that, your clients will recommend you to other clients. Every new successful project contributes to your reputation. Project by project, assignment by assignment, you will be building your own prestige; your work becomes a reflection of who you are.

This means that just as successful and impressive projects reflect on you, so do mistakes, which can be challenging, but remember: mistakes are opportunities for learning. Some of the best and most memorable moments of my life have been connected to my studio and the projects I've done through it.

The Challenges of Freelancing

How you manage your time, how you talk to clients, and how you meet deadlines and your own goals, among many other things, defines your work culture. Think of your studio or business as if it were a person: Is it respectful? Is it organized, or is it chaotic? Does it meet the deadlines it sets for itself? Is it smiling or serious? Kind or bitter? All of these qualities define the culture of your practice and the type of professional you want to be. And your work culture will be expressed through the quality of the work you do, your daily exchange with clients and collaborators, your commitment to projects, your working hours, and your rules and processes.

Your work culture is unique and fits who you are and your way of being. This is what will make you stand out in the crowd.

Managing Working Hours

Time management is one of the essential ingredients to your success as a freelancer. This includes not only how long your work day lasts, if you work Monday to Friday or take Friday off, and when you take holidays, but also how you manage your day-to-day tasks.

When you don't have someone else organizing your day, it's easy to let hours slip by doing irrelevant tasks, ending your workday without having achieved any specific goal. Determine overarching goals as well as other, more concrete goals; completing the latter will help you to fill in the big picture.

Having the ability to work fast is definitely a plus. That doesn't mean you should always do it, but if you're able to tackle certain jobs quickly, it can leave a positive impression on your clients and benefit your business. By establishing processes and rules for yourself, you can increase your speed and effectiveness. In addition, with tried and true methods, you won't waste time reinventing the wheel every time you have to complete an assignment.

That said, keep your eye out for assignments with unrealistic deadlines. Projects like this can easily turn into an incomplete job that neither you nor your client are satisfied with. A project that you can't include in your portfolio has certainly much less reward than one that you can. Remember that the job you are doing now might bring you more work in the future—the better the result, the better future assignments will be.

Managing Free Time

Managing free time as a freelancer is complex. The line between working too much and too little is a fine one, and can have a direct impact on your income. It's so easy as the only one responsible for getting your projects done to find yourself working after hours or canceling a dinner because "the files sent to the printer had a mistake." Or you may, without considering the implications, plan a long vacation during a time of the year when many assignments tend to come your way. Poorly planned time off can have adverse effects on your year-round income.

It cannot be said too many times: as a freelancer you are both boss and employee. Embracing both roles simultaneously can help guide you in many of your business decisions and find the answer to many of your questions. As a boss, think about how much vacation time you would give an employee. Likewise, think about how much vacation time you would like to have as an employee. The number of days off you should take is probably an average of the two.

Monthly Goals — April 2030

General
– Update the website
– Organize materials and storage
– Prepare workspace

New projects
– Write *The Big Leap 2*

Education
– New Letter&Co. display type design course
– Online seminar on lettering

Administration
– Incorporate time tracking

Some time ago I started using a document called monthly goals. There I write down all the things I want to achieve during the month. One example follows: update my website. In this file I also write down the tasks I want to accomplish each week in order to achieve that monthly goal. In this way, my day-to-day work is not dictated by those things that I remember or that I spontaneously feel like doing. I have pre-established tasks based on my larger goals. This saves me a lot of time down the line and has a reward: the great pleasure of the goal achieved. Working with goals even when you are working on your own is very rewarding (and effective)!

I remember when I used to work as an employee, I dreamed of being able to take a long vacation and travel the world. Today, with my own studio, I travel the world working and, paradoxically, I rarely take vacations that last more than fifteen days.

The fact is that a long vacation is associated with considerable loss of revenue. However, I have been able to organize my assignments in a way that allows me to visit other cities. Being a freelancer gives me the power to do something I had long dreamed of: to travel the world.

The Tasks of a Freelancer

You are a business owner! But you are also an employee—the only one (for now). That means that you will not only be performing the creative work, but covering all the administrative tasks that your work involves. You will be in charge of positioning your brand and putting it "out there"; you will update your website, write newsletters, and/or design promotional material; you will go to networking events to meet new colleagues and potential collaborators; you may pick up the phone or write an e-mail to clients you want to do work for. When an assignment comes in, you'll be happy, and then you'll spend several hours preparing a quote. If approved, you will start with the conception and creative execution of the assignment and, if necessary, take care of the production aspects, sending a job to the printer or creating a prototype. Once finished, you will be happy with the result (and, of course, you will have to upload it to your website soon) and you will write the invoice. Make sure that it gets paid, and be mindful that, after expenses, you are turning a profit. Oh, and by the way, the printer has run out of paper and there's no more coffee: you'll have to take care of that, too.

In this section there's a breakdown of the basic tasks of a freelancer (see page 22). This will vary depending on the work you do. Does it seem like a lot? At times it is, but don't panic. Not every day is so full of activities, and behind every task there's the satisfaction of doing things your way.

Establishing Your Procedures

To define your procedures, you must, as I've said, think as both boss and employee. If you did have employees, what work would you still want to do yourself? If you were an employee, what rules would you find fair and useful? Considering both perspectives will help you establish an ideal set of procedures for working on your own.

Defining some procedures is essential to having a structure, otherwise you may lose control or simply waste time thinking of solutions each time you have to do a recurring task. Procedures cover various aspects of your practice, from the hours and days you work and the way you deliver a final job, to how you write an e-mail in a given situation. Stipulating some rules ensures that you won't reinvent the wheel every time you sit down at your desk.

For example, you can establish procedures for recurring tasks. You can specify how you write the first contact e-mail, how many days after the confirmation of the order you will deliver sketches, by what means you will deliver the final files, and when you will invoice for the work. In this way, once an assignment comes in, you know the steps you have to follow and you can spend your time doing creative work.

A client hires you not only because they like what you do, but also because they like how you work. If the client likes how you carry out the assignment and manage the project, he or she will come back for more, hoping that the next project will be managed in a similar way.

Being predictable in your professionalism is positive for you as well as for the client. Following a repeatable process will give you more space to do your best work—explosive, surprising, innovative, and new!

Variable Income

This is one of the main concerns of those thinking about becoming a freelancer. A fixed salary, which we have when we are working for someone else, provides a sense of security, a guarantee that we will have a known amount of money at a known date on a regular basis.

As a freelancer, you have the potential to earn much more than you used to earn as an employee, but your income will probably not be as consistent. There will be months of more work and months of less work. There will be months in which you will work a lot and earn little, and there will be other times when working just a few days will turn a profit to cover your expenses for several months. Keep track of which months are most productive, or the months in which you receive more orders, as this annual fluctuation often repeats as a pattern. This will help you organize other aspects of your life, such as when to take a vacation, start a personal project, or look for collaborators to help you get future work done.

Take advantage of the times when your clients take a break. For example, in Germany, where I live, almost all companies and agencies close during the week between the December holidays and New Year's Day. It's a given that during that time people take vacations or spend those days doing personal projects. In countries where the fiscal calendar closes in December and companies want to spend what they have left of their budgets, those same weeks can be very busy. If you live somewhere where that's the case, like the US, you'll have the opportunity to get a lot of commissions. Identifying high- and low-activity periods can help you plan your yearly calendar and make the most of your productive time.

Allocating Your Income

This seems like a very obvious thing, but it's not: Having more income will allow you to invest more (spend more on your business) and therefore generate even *more* income. If you don't invest time and money in reaching new customers and generating opportunities, you won't have enough income to cover your expenses.

That said, your expenses should also be in line with your income, not exceed it. Having little income doesn't mean you can't invest, because investing doesn't necessarily involve large sums of money, or any money at all. As a freelancer, your time and skills are an important part of your capital. Sometimes "investing" in your business means a little bit of extra time.

I regularly print promotional material, such as simple postcards made with my own art. I send these to clients and give them away at conferences to attract the attention of my ideal clients. This is just one of the small investments I make that helps me put some of my work out there. It's affordable but has expanded my client base.

Basic Tasks of a Freelancer

1. Communication

— Positioning your brand
— Creating promotional material
— Updating your portfolio
— Managing social media networks
— Maintaining personal projects

2. Client Acquisition

— Networking
— Contacting potential clients
— Following up

3. Creative Work, Execution, and Delivery

— Executing assignments
— Incorporating feedback
— Making corrections
— Delivering final products

4. Production and Coordination

— Preparing material (e.g., original files for printing or prototypes for production)
— Coordinating timelines with third parties
— Controlling quality
— Supervising production

5. Quote Preparation

— Preparing estimates for potential clients
— Following up after sending an estimate
— Negotiating terms
— Signing contracts

6. Invoicing and Payments

— Invoicing and payment follow-up
— Paying invoices
— Preparing taxes

7. Administration

— Monitoring income and expenses
— Monitoring resources and acquiring new ones (e.g., buying software or coffee)
— Maintenance (e.g., workspace cleaning, answering the phone)

Ease In or Just Leap?

The big question among those thinking of becoming freelancers is this: when is the best time to do it? In response to this question, there are essentially two major lines of thought. One perspective advocates for setting a future start date and creating a plan so you'll be ready to make the leap at this self-assigned time. The other, which is a more gradual approach, suggests keeping your current day job, and adding in freelance work on the side.

In the first scenario, the insecurity of not having a consistent income can motivate you to set it all in motion. The fear of not being able to pay the bills may generate that extra adrenaline you need to get you out there seeking clients, connecting with others, and reaching out to your network. The biggest risk is that you could fall short and be unable to cover your expenses as quickly as you estimated.

In the second, you are making a gradual transition toward a freelance business. While you maintain a job that allows you to pay the bills, you dedicate your free time to building something new. In this case, you will probably have to be prepared to receive e-mails and calls from your freelance clients during your regular work schedule, and you will also have to sacrifice your free time to complete freelance projects. The biggest risk here is that it's easy to overdo it and miss out on rest in order to deliver jobs on time.

How you proceed is a very personal decision. You know better than anyone whether the pressure will work for you or against you. Or if the strategy of adding clients on the side while you keep your day job is doable and will allow you to grow your freelance business. Also, your personal situation, which is different for everyone, will play a part. You may have children, a partner to support you, a mortgage, or an expensive car payment. You may absolutely despise your current job. All these parameters will help you measure the risks and benefits for each strategy and help you make the decision for your next step. Having said that, neither approach guarantees success or predicts failure for your business.

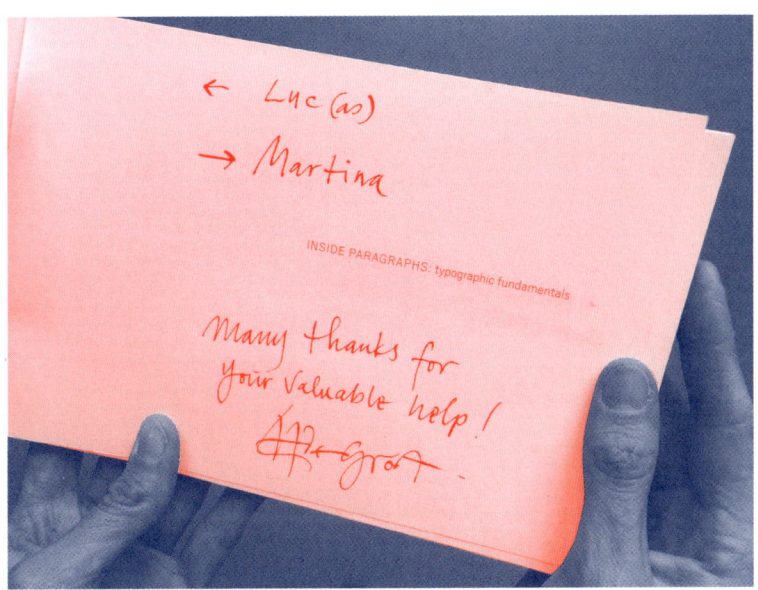

Being 100 percent committed to my practice and starting to look for clients was what finally launched my career as a freelancer. In my case, I did not set the date, but the date found me: I had finished an internship in a studio and unfortunately (or so I thought), they were not planning on hiring me as a permanent employee.

I still remember my last day as an employee, walking out the door of that studio with shaky legs, and a wonderful adventure ahead of me—though of course, I didn't know it then. Those shaky legs turned into energy, and two weeks later I was launching my new website and printing business cards. I was ready to tell the world what I wanted to do and that I was here and ready to do it.

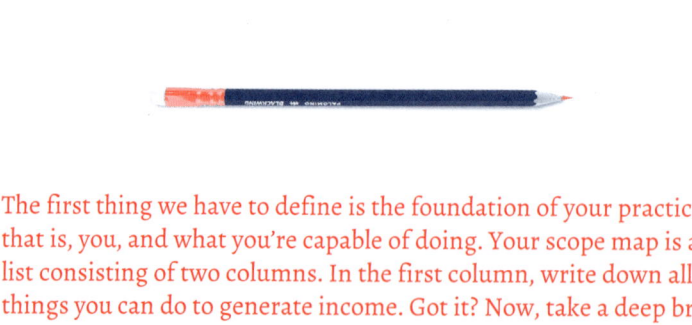

The first thing we have to define is the foundation of your practice: that is, you, and what you're capable of doing. Your scope map is a list consisting of two columns. In the first column, write down all the things you can do to generate income. Got it? Now, take a deep breath, close your eyes, and think about all the things that you'd really like to do from here on out. List those things in the second column. Now you have identified your true north: what you want for your business, and what tools you can use to get there.

What You Can Do	What You Want to Do

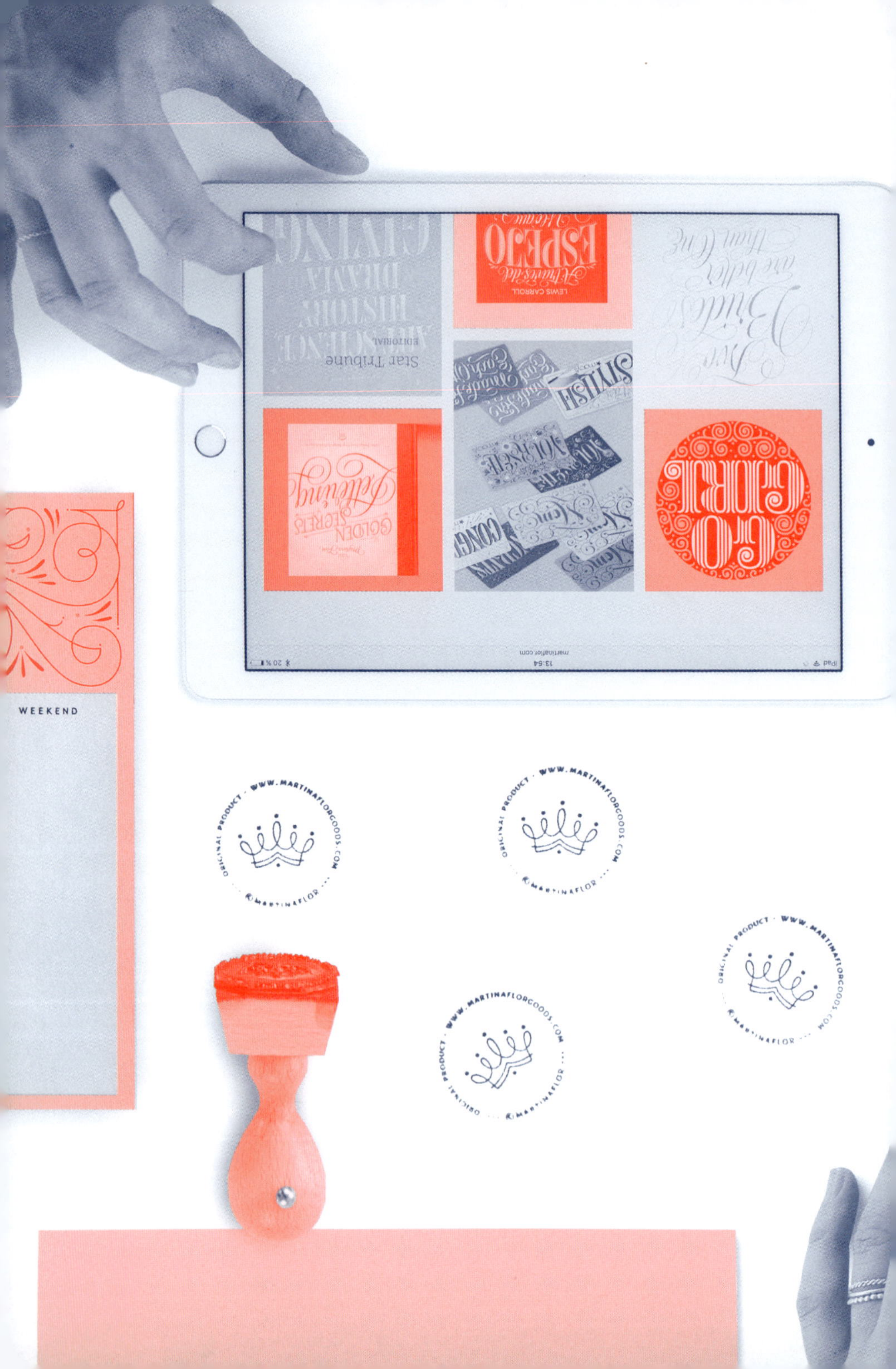
Star Tribune
EDITORIAL
LEWIS CARROLL
ESPEJO
STYLISH
martinaflor.com
13:54
WEEKEND
ORIGINAL PRODUCT · WWW.MARTINAFLORGOODS.COM · · · ©MARTINAFLOR

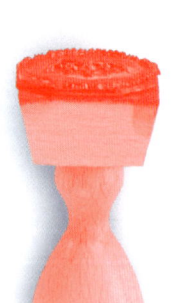

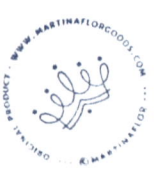

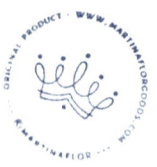

2. First Steps

Here we will talk about how to best present your work and expand your portfolio. We will also look at how to build your personal brand and present yourself appropriately, something essential to attracting the right assignments.

Your Professional Identity

As with brands and companies, you will also have an off-line and online presence. Your off-line presence comes through in your promotional materials and through how you present yourself: your attire, your office space, etc. Your online presence is shaped by your portfolio, your participation in social media, the e-mails you write, and more. Together with your work, all of these—off-line and on—form your identity and, therefore, it's important that both "presences" share some of the same language and have elements in common.

As a freelancer, it is not strictly necessary that you have a logo, but, if you choose to have one, it is important that the same version of your logo is used in all communication materials: business cards, website, e-mail signature, and any other promotional collateral (e.g., brochures, sell sheets). Something as simple as a color or typeface can help unify the look and feel of your identity, and ensure that everything appears to belong to the same business: yours.

Presenting Your Work

As a professional in the creative industries and visual disciplines, your work is your cover letter. Having a website or other type of online presence is important, not only for your potential clients, but also to position yourself within the market. Your site will be a personal space that shows what you are capable of, and ideally reflects the way you work.

A portfolio's purpose is twofold: (1) it shows potential clients the kind of work that you do (e.g., photography, illustration, branding, animation), and (2) it's a tool for keeping an updated overview of your work (i.e., a record of how it developed over time, and the type of commissions you have received). By looking at your portfolio you can understand your own trends (e.g., if you lean toward a certain color) and determine where you want to go with the assignments you take on.

Choose the Right Platform

There are basically two ways to have an online presence:
Participate in an online network for creative professionals: You can post your portfolio to a platform, such as Behance or Dribbble, to quickly and easily create a profile and upload your work. These are two among many networks that prospective clients visit to find creatives for particular jobs. To stay competitive on these sites it's important to participate in the community and keep your portfolio and personal information updated. One disadvantage of going this route is that these sites allow you only to post projects, so your clients won't be able to get a complete overview of your practice if, for example, you teach workshops or online classes.

Maintain a website with its own domain name: Creating a simple web page is, nowadays, within everyone's reach. There are many platforms and apps that are accessible to anyone who can find their way around a keyboard, and that help you with everything from registering your domain (i.e., your web address), to signing up for a hosting service (the space where your page will be hosted), to designing your site. Wordpress is one platform for creating your own site; it's free, relatively easy to use, and allows you to customize your website through themes or templates.

Build Your Portfolio for Your Ideal Client

Spend a few minutes thinking about who you want to work with. If, for example, you want to attract international clients, buy a .com or .net domain, which are the generic international domains. If your ideal client speaks English, don't spend time making your website available in German, Spanish, Bengali, and Turkish. Narrowing down these parameters will save you lots of work when it comes to choosing your domain name, your hosting service, and how you update your website.

Choose a Suitable Layout

You'll want your website—no matter which platform you use—to be easy to update, easy to navigate, and ideal for showcasing your best and most recent work. Forget about complex animations and text effects. Focus on showing your content as professionally and simply as possible. The design of the site itself should not drag any attention away from the projects you showcase, which need to shine.

Keep It Clear

Visitors to your website must be able to tell right away where they are, who you are, and how they can get to where they need to go on your site. Make it easy for them to find the navigation menu that will guide them through the content. There should be a section on your site that houses your work, an "about" page with a short biography, and your contact information. If you also do other things, such as teach in-person workshops, lead online courses, offer speaking engagements, or have an online shop, these should be included in the menu.

Show Recent Work

Keep your online portfolio up-to-date. This will help you secure new clients for the coming months and years. Try to include the process of updating your portfolio within your workflow, so that when you finish an assignment, in addition to invoicing, you make sure to upload it to your portfolio. It's good to keep in mind that the best etiquette is to wait to post a project until the client makes it public. Refrain from showing works in progress on your social media networks or in your portfolio. Most clients will prefer that you keep things under wraps until the project is live.

Present Your Work as Projects

Introduce yourself as someone who goes beyond making "beautiful images": you are a conceptual thinker with a creative personality, and that should also be reflected in your portfolio. Ideally, write a note about each project describing the task, the creative process, and its inspiration; don't forget to give credit to anyone you've worked with on the project (e.g., art directors, editors). Include links to your clients' websites as well: what goes around comes around!

Edit Your Work

Your portfolio should reflect the type of work you want to do in the future, and should not be a document of all of the work you've done. You no longer want to do calligraphed wedding cards? Then don't include the invitations you made for your cousin's wedding. If there is a job that you accepted only to pay the bills and you are not proud of the result, don't show it on your website. The basic rule is: don't show any work you don't like, just those things you would like to do more of.

Make People Visit Your Portfolio

Once you have your portfolio online you must find ways to get people to see it. If it is hosted on a network, then you should become active in that network. If you have an independent website, you should look for other ways to drive traffic to it. As part of this strategy, include your web address in all your printed promotional material as well as digital communications (e.g., e-mail signature, contact card, Twitter, and/or Instagram). Additionally, join the creative community in some way. Art directors, designers, and gallery owners are much more likely to get to you indirectly than by happening upon your website.

People work with people they like, and that may start with a like on Instagram, a comment on your blog, or a chat at a networking dinner. Find your own ways to make yourself visible: go to design conferences or meetings, stay active on different online channels. My recommendation is that you try different platforms and check what each brings you and which one you enjoy the most. It may seem like a lot of work—and it is—but it's worth it and it can even be fun.

Measure Your Efforts

If you decide to build your own website, you might want to track your web traffic. How can you track the success of a certain promotion you've done and know if it really drove traffic to your site? Fortunately, there are tools on web platforms that will inform you about all of this. For example, by including a simple Google Analytics code on your website, you'll get a lot of insights about your most visited projects, where traffic comes from, and what kind of audience is interested in your work.

Social Media Networks: To Join or Not to Join?

The work of a freelancer can be quite lonely. While you often work with clients, art directors, and editors, it's likely that most of your time will be spent on your own in front of your computer or in your workspace.

Joining social media networks has helped me find a balance: they keep me in daily contact with people who are interested in what I do, and this encourages me to keep working and keep improving. Of course, the danger is that social media networks can also distract me and sometimes take up more time than I would like. But to tell the truth, without social media networks I would find other ways to waste time. Many publishers and art directors use social media networks to look for new talent, so staying active on them might also create your next job opportunity. In chapter 4 we will talk about social media networks in detail and the best ways to participate.

Building a Solid Portfolio and Being Your Own Client

As freelancers, the most important thing we have is our portfolio. It reflects our expertise and the quality of what we do, and it is what attracts the attention of clients. That said, when we are just starting out, we might not yet have a large portfolio of work that shows what we're capable of.

To build an attractive portfolio we need commissions, and to get commissions we need a solid portfolio: a circle that has no end. But I have good news: there are ways to create work without client assignments—you can expand your portfolio with personal or self-initiated projects and collaborations.

To do these kinds of projects you don't need a professional assignment, but only to invest your time (and sometimes money, if possible). The disadvantage is also a great advantage: the absence of a client.

Self-Initiated Projects

A self-initiated project is one that you do on your own, to explore certain techniques, skills, or concepts out of interest, without having a commission triggering it. Since you are not limited to a brief, you can create impactful pieces that showcase your skills and talents. However, self-initiated projects can be challenging because you don't have an external deadline or a client waiting in anticipation for the work to get done. It's easier to give up before you've finished.

For a self-initiated project, I offer the following guidelines to ensure your success in finishing and posting your project: create a brief, set a deadline, and post the final product.

A brief is a defined set of essential parameters, usually supplied by a client. In this case it can be something like: I will draw one object per day (if illustration is your thing), or, I will take one portrait per day (if you work with photography). The more defined this brief, the more powerful the result.

If, as a photographer, you decide to take portraits, it'll be harder to differentiate your project from many other portrait projects out there. But if you want to take portraits of elderly women wearing their wedding dresses, there's more of a chance that your project will stand out as unique.

Your brief shouldn't be so complicated, however, that it takes up a lot of your time. Remember: as a freelancer you'll also have to carry out commercial work that generates income. Try to keep this brief short, simple, and doable.

Once your brief is clear and well-defined, decide how quickly you should have the piece finished: whether it's in one hour, three hours, or four days. You need to set a time frame for the work, and you need to know when you will stop working on it, even if the project is not done. Deadlines have an important impact on our productivity, and training ourselves in this productivity is part of our skill set as freelancers.

Finally, share your work. Sharing your work has two positive aspects: (1) it creates extra pressure to complete the piece in a reasonable amount of time, and (2) it can attract prospective clients who need similar work done. There are numerous ways you can share your work, as discussed above: blog, social media networks, your online portfolio…

Collaborations

A collaboration involves partnering with someone who complements you in some way, a relationship in which you contribute something that the other lacks and vice versa. The sum, as the saying goes, is often greater than the parts; both artists benefit from the work of the other.

If you are a pattern designer, for example, you can collaborate with a fabric manufacturer, and together create a line of fabrics with your designs. The producer will contribute their expertise and infrastructure to create and print fabrics; you will contribute your know-how to create attractive and innovative patterns. Together, you will create a line of distinctive fabrics. Without one or the other, this would not be possible.

A successful collaboration requires mutual trust, a fair profit split, and an equal desire to share the results. Your collaborator must be someone you admire and consider competent at what they do, as they will have equal influence on the project.

When I started my lettering studio, I didn't have many projects in my portfolio that had to do with letters, so I had to create projects that would expand my portfolio and improve my skills. That's how I decided to start with letteringvscalligraphy.com, a project that I initiated with the calligrapher Giuseppe Salerno in which we challenged each other with our skills in an online battle. The home page was divided in two: on the left there was lettering, and on the right calligraphy. Each day we uploaded a letter executed with our own technique: Giuseppe with calligraphy (writing the letter), and me with lettering (drawing the letter). There was a guest moderator who would suggest an attribute to be incorporated into our brief—a "sensual S," for example.

The hook of the site was that people could vote for the work they liked best. The project went viral, and on its first day online we received seven thousand unique visits. Every day an average of two thousand people visited to vote for their favorite artistic rendering of that day's letter. Giuseppe experimented with different calligraphic tools, different supports and papers, and sometimes wrote without ink by using his finger on the touch screen of his smartphone. I tried different ways of drawing letters: sometimes the letters were traditional, sometimes abstract, at times an illustration or an object. We had fun while expanding our skill sets and, at the same time, our portfolios.

The essential parts of a self-initiated project were there: we had a brief (to execute a letter with an attribute), a deadline (we had to produce one letter per day in a maximum of one or two hours), and we shared, through networks and, of course, on the project's website. This project helped me build my portfolio as well as my confidence: I demonstrated to the world what I could do, but above all I proved it to myself.

A suitable collaborator will admire your work as much as you admire theirs. You'll also want to be able to trust the other party to pull their creative weight to ensure that it will be a true collaboration.

In the previous example, you and your collaborator might decide to sell the line of textiles you created together. Each of you should then collect profits equivalent or proportional to the work you did. In other words, profits must be shared. It's best if you and your collaborator are at a similar stage in your careers; this will create the best conditions for working together. If you collaborate with a company that is much larger than yours, you might have to insist that the profit from the collaboration is split fairly.

Finally, sharing the results of your collaboration is crucial if you want to attract new commissions or get more mileage out of your design. The patterns you designed for this line of textiles can turn into a line of wallpaper, wrapping paper, or mugs. Don't forget to include it all in your portfolio, share on your social media networks, and request samples for your own archive.

Decorata is a font I created in collaboration with Positype. They contributed their expertise in creating and selling fonts, and I contributed art direction and the design of an original alphabet. Both parties receive a percentage of sales.

Introducing Yourself

Your "About" Page

The "About" page is an important part of your portfolio. If you are not able to define yourself then others will not be able to either. An "About" page has important information about who you are and how to contact you.

The person who hires you for a certain job will do it not only for the quality of the work they see in your portfolio, but also because you seem to be the ideal person to carry out the project they need done in a creative, enjoyable, and effective way.

A proper "About" page includes the following:

Your contact information: This is very important. Your contact information should be visible and highlighted. You don't want a potential client to have to work or invest any extra time in looking for how to reach you. You may also add this information at the footer or header of your website.

A profile picture: Nowadays, assignments are mostly discussed by e-mail. We rarely get to know the person who's hiring us, so it is more meaningful than ever to showcase the person behind the website. Those of us working with images know the power they have, so it is important to choose them carefully. Ideally, the photo you use is one that's taken specifically to be paired with your bio. It's usually obvious when the image used is out of context. That photo you took looking gorgeous on your last beach holiday? Probably not the one you should use with your bio—even if you crop out that beach umbrella. Similarly, avoid family photos (regardless of whether your family is important to you) and any other images that offer too many specifics and too much context. Your profile picture should be about you and you alone.

A bio: The first thing to decide is whether you will speak in the first person or not; for example: "Hello, my name is Becca, and I am a graphic designer with an expertise in editorial design." As a general rule, the first person sounds more active and casual because you are talking directly to the reader. The third person reads as if someone else is introducing you: "Becca is a graphic designer with expertise in editorial design." This

Whenever I visit a site, I look at the "About" page after scrolling through the portfolio. A very limited or poorly constructed bio comes across as unfriendly.

Your portfolio is a very personal space, almost like your living room. Make a good impression by introducing yourself appropriately and welcoming visitors in.

voice gives the impression of formality. Both are valid for your bio, and you can choose the one that you feel best represents you.

Your Bio

Your bio should include the following:

What you do: Share plainly and simply what you do. Visitors to your website must immediately understand whether they have entered the website of a graphic designer, a tea house, or a medical center. First, describe yourself in a few words: "My name is Milo and I am a photographer specializing in product photography and advertising." Clarify who you are from the start so visitors know they are in the right place, stay on your site, and read the rest of your bio.

Your most important degrees and credentials: Give insights about the kind of training you've had. If you went to university, specify which one and what courses you took— "I started my design studies at Parsons School of Design in New York. Three years later, I moved to the Netherlands to specialize in type design." If you are self-taught, include the courses you have taken, or the experiences that have allowed you to develop in your field— "I have traveled the world photographing cities and nature. That's how my love for landscape photography was born." Your expertise is not something you necessarily learned in a school or university. Probably, other experiences have left a mark on the way you do things, and these anecdotes become what distinguishes you— "I discovered that I wanted to be an illustrator when, by chance, I began creating portraits for my friends in my free time."

Your target audience: Do you work locally or internationally? You don't need to list your clients here, but you can be specific about the types of clients for whom you typically work: "I work for agencies and publishing houses inside and outside the United Kingdom," or "I work with cultural and state institutions in the United States."

Related activities: All the work you do in and around your field differentiates you from other professionals and adds to your professional value. You don't have to list all the ceramic courses you've taken, or mention that you like to do CrossFit on Saturdays, but all activities that are related to your profession define you and have a place here.

Your strengths: Do you have a special aptitude for project management? Are you skilled at creating editorial illustrations for small formats? Are your black-and-white photographs very

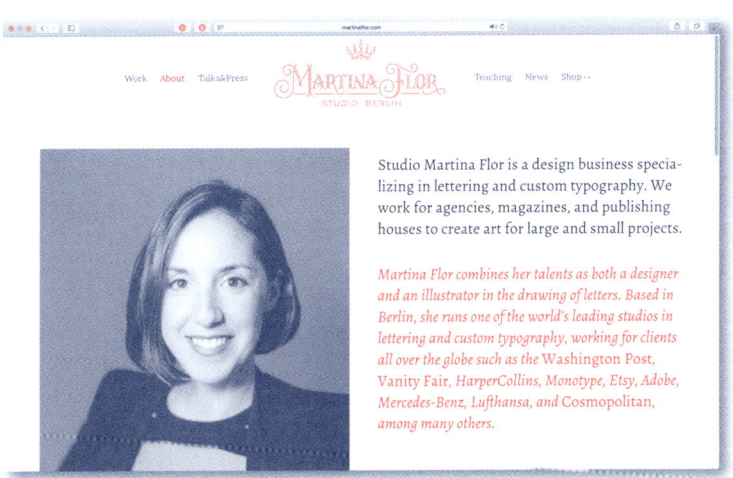

In my bio, I mention that, in addition to drawing letters (my main expertise), I speak at conferences, teach workshops, lead online classes, and carry out self-initiated projects. These experiences and activities enrich my work and therefore make it more attractive for potential clients.

impactful? Then write about it in your bio. Talk about your strengths—that is, highlight general qualities without becoming too specific. Writing "I am skilled at drawing birds resting on the branches of trees in New York City" would pigeonhole you into doing that and only that.

Select clients: List only those clients that are easily recognizable. This will give you credibility and speak to your reputation. If you have medium-to-large clients, or smaller clients that are relevant to the field you're working in, list them.

Social media networks you're a part of: A potential client may have found your site, but it is very unlikely that she will visit it often to check if you have updated it or added projects to your portfolio. Make it easy for her to follow you on a social media network. This will increase the chances that she will stay up-to-date with your work (if, of course, you post regularly).

While these are the basic ingredients for your "About" page, you will find your own way to shape it. The important thing is that it is a pleasant, swift read, and gives a clear overview of who you are and the work that you do. You can give it a clever slant that helps make the information more digestible, and you can also give it a personal touch by adding something like a "Ten facts about myself" section, including a photo of the first time you grabbed a brush, or featuring the last three photos you uploaded to Instagram. Let your "About" page reveal a little bit about the person behind the work.

Use this worksheet to craft your bio. Before you try explaining to the world who you are and what you do, you should spend a little time clarifying it for yourself. Writing a bio is a bit like executing a project—it's easiest if you're following a brief. I've listed some of the important topics you need to address to create your own bio. Of course, you are the one who decides what is redundant and how extensive your bio should be.

What You Do

Your Degrees and Credentials

Your Target Audience

Related Activities

Your Strengths

Select Clients

Social Media Networks

Your Contact Information

3. Generating Income

In this chapter, we will look at possible income streams in detail as well as the challenges and advantages of each. We'll also talk about how to build an audience and develop a network of connections for selling your work.

Income Streams

We tend to think of a freelancer as someone who works on her own and offers services. Although it is true that working with clients is one of the most common ways for freelancers to earn money, I have liberating news for you: it is not the only way.

As a freelancer you can do commissions for clients or you can teach other people to do what you do. You can also create products and sell them. You can even do all of these things at once.

Nowadays freelancers have an additional scenario: the power to build their very own audience through social networks, one that consumes the products they create, whether that's an online class, a digital product, or an object.

There are those who believe that the best thing is to "diversify" your income, so that you are not dependent on a single income stream—if one income stream is slow, you can rely on the others. There are some, on the other hand, who think it's best to focus on one thing. Aside from the theories, what you must always keep in mind is that you are in search of what works best for you. You get to shape your business around your way of being and living. In other words, you need to find a way to proceed in your freelance venture that you enjoy, that fits who you are, and that makes your career and work life sustainable.

Client Commissions

Generally, when you are working with clients, you will work on a project basis. A client will approach you with a project; you will respond with a quote or estimate for the job at hand, plan it, execute it, implement it, and, finally, invoice it.

Challenges

Working for clients means first and foremost working with people. This can, of course, be a positive experience, but it also has its challenges. Your client is entrusting you with a project and paying for your services, and it's important to maintain a good balance of professionalism and kindness. Just as you do your best to work effectively and efficiently with your clients, your clients are, we hope, doing their best to work effectively and efficiently with you. Part of your service is to make sure you have a crystal clear brief, and that you and your client are in agreement about what the deliverables are and their respective deadlines. Your job is to also help organize the work for your client, so that her experience of working with you feels easy and smooth, and is not something she has to "struggle" with or worry about.

Nobody likes to work with unclear (or grumpy!) people. Your clients don't necessarily have to know about typography, rules of composition, or color theory. But should they have questions about what you've done, you can spend a minute answering them in a friendly and accessible way so they might understand why you've made the creative decisions you've made—and accept these changes in your design or illustration with a smile. After all, you and your client are looking for the same thing: an outstanding result.

Another challenge of client work lies in confronting its fluctuation. There will be weeks or months when you will have your hands full of projects and deadlines, and weeks or months when you will be sitting and waiting (in a metaphorical sense, because, as you will learn, there is always work to be done when you're freelance!). That means revenue will fluctuate too. Some jobs will pay the bills for three months, while others will not generate substantial income.

In every field, there are months that are regularly more intense than others. Keep track of how your workload fluctuates, so as not to despair when work diminishes. And don't worry—these fluctuations are nothing to worry too much about—you'll find out why next.

Advantages

Good news! Work for clients can potentially pay very well. That means that the months you have less work can be funded by the months that you have more. Of course, this depends on the kinds of clients with whom you work, and your potential to earn more or less according to your reputation. The truth is that work for clients is made and paid for in a more or less short period of time. And, if you prepare well, it can even generate profits (passive income) afterward, something I'll address later.

Trainings and Workshops

Whether you'd like to teach workshops depends entirely on you. You'll need a concept or idea, a physical space in which to hold the workshop, and a plan for promoting it. Of course, the great fear that underlies any workshop that you'll have no sign-ups, especially if it's your very first one. The more specific you are in naming the goal of your workshop, the more it will stand out. If you are an illustrator, for example, you might want to teach watercolor painting, or drawing faces or animals. Specific goals will help differentiate your class from more general classes on illustration.

You will also need a schedule and a description of how the workshop will develop—either over a period of hours or weeks, depending. You will need to specify why people should sign up for your class, what they will gain from the experience, and what they will leave the class with (e.g., three small paintings, a collection of five photographs they can add to their portfolio, etc.). You will need to reserve a physical space suitable for the class, where you and the attendees can work comfortably. Finally, you will need a place where people can register. You can use your own website or a platform, such as Eventbrite, which, although it charges you a small fee for each ticket sold, also allows for your event to be listed on a platform with a broad following, and makes the whole process much easier for you.

Teaching can be a healthy source of income, as well as a good way to perfect your own creative techniques. It can also help you improve your communication skills and increase your self-confidence—in your classes, you get to play the expert, because you are!

The first workshop I taught, I offered for free—I thought of it as a practice run, where I could put myself to the test and confirm if I was any good at teaching lettering. The workshop went very well. For the first time, I experienced something that is probably what makes me want to continue teaching to this day: I could tell that people left the workshop feeling truly inspired. They were seeing typography in a different way and were going to be able to use what they learned in their creative work. After that experience, I continued organizing work-shops, but usually in spaces that already had a calendar of activities. I gave those venues a percentage of my total profits from registrations, but they provided the space and marketed to their audience. Later, I started taking my work-shops to other cities, and I coordinated them together with a range of venues. Nowadays, my workshops are an important part of my work and my income, and my experience doing them over the years has allowed me to lead trainings for creative teams in companies and agencies, as well as teach at universities. Moreover, teaching workshops is a good way to get to know your own creative process, which, as we will see later, may help you to better work with clients.

Challenges

Teaching workshops can be a very rewarding experience. Just as with your clients, you need to know how to identify what your students might be looking for and what they need most from you. Teaching can, in this way, require quite a bit of energy. You must have the ability to offer quick solutions to various problems. In addition, your attendees will have different levels of expertise, so you will have to be patient and learn to accommodate this—it requires a certain amount of improvisation and thinking on your feet. This is challenging, but something you will get better and better at the more you teach.

Finally, you need to learn to nurture an audience for your workshops, which takes time and won't happen overnight. Sometimes, word of mouth will become your best marketing strategy (that requires no work on your part!). You have to make sure, though, that attendees are having positive experiences. By creating attractive, fun, informative, and well-structured workshops, you will ensure value and take-aways for your students. Additionally, being creative with your promotions both online and off-line, especially at the beginning, or if you are teaching in a new venue or city, is key—and will take time.

Advantages

Teaching positions you as an expert. Those attending your workshops are likely to be professionals in your field, and will likely include people who may hire you at some point in the future.

Teaching allows you to showcase your experience and know-how (whether you draw, take photos, or do graphic design) and help others get better at it. You will increase and elevate your professional reputation, demonstrate how fun and fulfilling it can be to work in your field, and give students the tools they need to get started. Regarding the profit, workshops may pay well in relation to the amount of time invested (normally a full day). However, you may not have frequent opportunities to conduct one-off workshops unless you diversify the content of your classes and cover different topics.

Speaking Engagements

Speaking at conferences is a good way to showcase your work and build a network. If you're good at it, it can even become an income stream. Developing an interesting talk on a topic or on your own work is tricky as it requires the combination of a good story or engaging content, complementary and interesting visuals, and the skills to deliver both. Combining all these elements into a solid and inspiring presentation requires both effort and time.

If you have a talent for public speaking you're ahead of the pack, but if you don't have that yet, don't worry—it's something you can learn. Finding your personal voice for presenting is a skill that develops through time and repeated experiences. If you are interested in trying it, you can start by identifying those presentations that have captivated you and analyze why: What was special in that storyline? What did you like about the

I have given talks at conferences for audiences ranging from fifty to ten thousand people, and in every one of them I have felt the adrenaline rush of getting onstage.

Public speaking can be fabulous, because through it you can make an impact on other people and change their way of seeing the world—that's powerful!

visuals? What did you notice about the body language of the speaker? If speaking is something you end up enjoying, then it can become part of your work. The better your presentations, the more conferences will want to have you, and oftentimes they will offer you a fee to talk.

Challenges

Giving a talk can be an act of vulnerability, and the great challenge is to make the audience leave your talk somehow transformed—even if that just means leaving them with a new idea they are turning over in their minds. Of course, this isn't easy. Seen in this way, when you give a talk, you are a facilitator of information—you are passing it along, sharing your wisdom and experience—and not the star of a show. You will need to make an experience of yours connect with the audience, so that it becomes useful to them in their own life and work. Ideally, your presentations should not be a mere portfolio presentation (the audience can visit your website for that), but something more personal and inviting. A talk called "Ten Years of Designing Logos" doesn't sound as appealing as "The Three Logos That Made Me Grow as a Designer." A good way to find an attractive topic for a talk is to focus on the particular rather than the general, and to use your own experience as a trigger for a lesson or revelation.

Talks are generally comprised of spoken and visual content, and they must complement each other. Your talk is a staging of what you have to say (and how you say it) and what you have to share or show (and how you show it).

Another challenge of giving talks is the difficulty of speaking in front of a large audience. Not everyone is born with the gift of public speaking skills, including the perfect body language for every punch line. Depending on our weaknesses and strengths, we can put more or less attention into practicing those aspects of our presentation. My advice is to present it several times to colleagues and friends and observe their reactions, and also to ask them what works and what does not. Ask for feedback and evolve your talk over time based on the feedback you receive.

You might shorten, revise, and adjust your talk depending on how much time you are allotted (once you have a venue), and the context of the presentation.

Advantages

Presenting at conferences and events often involves traveling, and hopefully this experience, apart from connecting you with new people, will take you to new places. Although some conferences do not offer a speaker fee, many do. As a freelancer you can take on as many speaking engagements as you like, as long as they don't take too much time away from your main assignments.

Finally, speaking positions you in the forefront of your own industry, and as a result you will gain recognition from your peers as well as potential clients.

Online Classes

Offering online classes is another great option for applying and benefiting from your work and expertise. An online class can be a video or a series of videos in which you show the process for carrying out a certain task—it can also be streamed live. The processes are explained in such a way that the students can execute them in steps, following your instruction. Generally, online classes are project-oriented so that students can apply a particular technique or new skill in executing their own project.

If you are interested in teaching online, you will need to develop content, record the lessons, edit the material, and post. The time you want to invest in creating the videos depends on you—today, with a smartphone camera and a microphone you can make very decent videos. What is really essential is that the content of your videos is understandable and clear.

There are several options for setting up online classes: first, you can offer them on your website and have them accessible for a fee. Or you can create a YouTube channel and offer them for free. The former allows you to generate income, and the latter can help you build a bigger audience for your work, products, skills, and future fee-based workshops. There are also a variety of online learning platforms. The big advantage of using one of these for your course is that they already have an audience, and will allow people to find your class more easily. Some of them, like Skillshare or Udemy, allow you to upload your own videos; others, like Domestika, film their own classes and handpick their teachers. All of them offer royalties in exchange for content, which vary according to the number of students and how successful the class is. Some of them even measure your success according to how engaging your class is and how many minutes were watched.

My online classes offer a different venue for sharing my skills with others, outside of in-person workshops and giving talks. These classes do not compete with my in-person offerings, and through them I can travel virtually to other cities and countries. They help me expand my audience and connect with other creatives.

The good news is that online classes produce passive income, which means that once the class is online, you will receive monthly royalties. You will get paid without working.

Challenges

Online classes present similar challenges to workshops: you have to thoughtfully elaborate on your subject and communicate your expertise in an interesting way for your class to be successful. The more distinctive the subject, the more likely you are to solve a particular audience problem. "Learn to Use Photoshop," for example, is perhaps too broad a class topic. "Creating Smart Masks with Photoshop," on the other hand, might solve a specific problem for your students and tangibly enhance their workflow.

If you choose to offer online classes, you will need to periodically answer your students' questions— an investment of time.

As with all internet content, when it comes to online classes, novelty wins the day. This means that you'll need to generate content regularly so that your classes don't become outdated.

Advantages

Welcome to the world of passive income—you'll love it! Passive income is money that makes itself. Of course, passive income streams require an initial investment of your time—you'll need to generate the content you're going to sell—but when all is said and done you will receive a monthly, quarterly, semiannual, or annual royalties check.

Of course, the income an online class generates can also fluctuate. If, for example, you offer a class on "How to Light Couples Portraits," you will perhaps get the most sign-ups before the wedding season, or around Valentine's Day. That said, the big advantage of generating passive income streams is that they will supplement your earnings as a freelancer, helping you cover a range of expenses, such as the rent for your workspace.

Creating and Selling Products

In the same way that you create a product when you execute an assignment for a client, you can create a product without an assignment and offer it for sale to potential customers. In the first case, the client is making the financial investment in what is being produced, and in the second case, you are.

Depending on the project, the investment will be larger or smaller. If you are an illustrator, you can, for example, create prints of your work. You would have to invest your time preparing the image or illustration, and perhaps pay for the production of the prints. You could choose to print on demand, which would reduce your investment to only the time spent

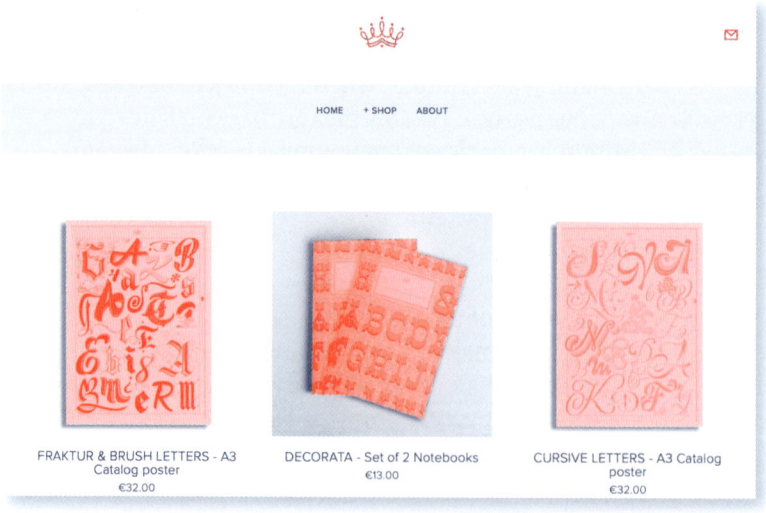

My product line is composed of items featuring my typography and lettering. My followers and type aficionados are my customers. Selling online has a very different rhythm than client work. Demand for products often corresponds to special events and holidays, such as Mother's Day and Christmas.

on the artwork. There are endless product possibilities when repurposing your creative work—calendars, greeting cards, card decks, coasters, and more.

You can offer these products in your own online shop, at appropriate stores, and at art and design fairs, or sell them during other events, such as at your workshops.

In all cases, you should not underestimate the complexity of making a product, as even the simplest one requires prototyping and testing. In addition, all products require packaging, no matter how simple, and storage space. If you have an online shop, bear in mind that you will have to process orders and ship them by post. If you sell at fairs, you will spend some time preparing for set-up, selling, and everything else involved in retail.

There are online platforms (like Society6 and Printful) where you provide the motif or the art, and they produce the products on demand and ship them to customers. If you go this route, you will receive only a small percentage of sales (around 10 percent on average).

Challenges

Running a profitable online shop is no small task, and the work required should not be underestimated. Producing a physical product can be complex and time-consuming. I suggest engaging strong and reliable collaborators (see page 36) and suppliers for each product you develop; they will help you create better pieces and make the process more enjoyable. Although an online shop can appear to be an avenue for earning passive income, it actually requires a lot of labor and maintenance. You need to attract visitors to your shop with a cohesive communication strategy. And once visitors arrive at your online shop, you'll want them to have a good buying experience, making their purchase easily and receiving it quickly. You'll need to plan ahead for problems that may arise during the delivery process, such as a lost or late package, or an order that has arrived incomplete, defective, or damaged. Alternatively, using an established online marketplace like Etsy or Zibbet can save you some time figuring all that out.

If you are creating a physical product, one thing to keep in mind when setting up an online shop is that a large percentage of your business depends on trustable, efficient shipping, so you'll want to make sure you have a reliable supplier—it will save you some big headaches.

Advantages

Creating a product is a truly magical process. What you conceived in two dimensions suddenly gains dimensionality and becomes an object. The satisfaction of walking down the street and seeing someone wearing a T-shirt with the print you designed or going to a conference and seeing someone wearing your pin is hard to describe. On the other hand, creating a product line is an absolutely holistic process— ranging from your brand's corporate identity to naming and packaging design—which is truly interesting and has the potential to be unique and stand out from other brands. Selling products has the potential to free you from client work: you will work independently and, ideally, become self-sufficient. In this case, your potential customer base grows as the potential of internet retail expands.

Licensing Art and Design

Each project you do, each piece, is created for a particular application. For example, as an advertising photographer you might take a photo for the cover of a company catalog. You will sign a contract, execute the assignment, and invoice for the work. The client, according to what has been agreed, might have licensed the photograph from you only for that particular use. In other words, if they would like to use your photo for something else, such as an advertising campaign, they must obtain a license for that particular use as well. This is an opportunity to make passive income from an image that you've already created.

I created this design for a client. Later, I was able to create silk-screen prints to sell in my shop. I recently collaborated with Tattly, a temporary tattoo company, which turned this design into one of their products, *for which I receive monthly royalties. Licensing your design allows you to get the most from your work in various applications and thus connect with more partners and markets.*

When taking on an assignment, it's vital that you come to a clear agreement with the client regarding the use of the resulting product *before beginning the project*. If your client wants to use the image you're creating in other ways than what the original assignment stipulates, and therefore make more revenue from it, you need to be sure that you get more revenue as well. As we will see later, the size of the project as well as the size of the client will affect the cost of any service, including that involved in licensing. It is not the same to create an illustration for a flyer with a print run of two hundred copies as it is to create one for a campaign that will wallpaper an entire city and also make print media and TV appearances. It is one thing to make an illustration for the owner of a shoe store in your neighborhood, and quite another to create one for a multinational brand of sports footwear.

Following this principle, the internet has created a whole new host of very accessible markets for licensing images, illustrations, and digital products. As a photographer, for instance, you can post your images for sale in an image bank;

as a calligrapher, you can create and sell different brushes for iPad or Adobe Illustrator; as an illustrator, you can sell your artwork to companies and publishers that print and sell postcards in the stationery market; as a designer, you can create a series of icons and make them available for download as vector drawings. These are just a few options. Anyone in the marketplace who needs these elements can buy a license according to the intended purpose and use them. The cost of that license—and thus your profit—will vary, depending on the number and type of applications. This way, instead of granting the license to a person (or firm) as in the case of an assignment, you will create the product and sell multiple licenses for its use.

There are several ways to market these kinds of products, and how you market will change according to the category of product it falls into. For example, some professionals create an online and printed catalog and offer it personally to their clients; others have a profile in an online marketplace and sell their products as digital downloads. Whatever the channel is, the positive thing about this type of revenue stream is that it requires only an initial investment on your part to create the product, and then an investment of time to make it available for licensing. Sales become passive revenue.

Challenges

Licensing art requires a great deal of knowledge about the costs involved in certain art licenses (an advertising campaign will involve a different fee than a series of mass-printed postcards), as well as knowledge of the appropriate contracts for each license. It's important and often necessary to seek out and take good advice from those who know before signing those contracts, so that you fully understand the financial agreement you are entering into. The field of licensing graphic materials, vector art, or photography online, through a service like Shutterstock, is easier to handle—each platform sets its own standards and takes care of the licensing for you. As a result, in exchange for relieving you of all administrative work, these channels retain a high percentage of your sales.

Advantages

Another passive income opportunity! And that's always something to celebrate. Of course, licensing art, photography, or graphic elements (to name a few) allows you to continue to benefit from a piece of your work. Have you ever made a design that was only printed fifty times? Or have you made a photo that only a few saw and you feel it is so unique that would you have liked to wallpaper the city with it? Licensing your work can open the door to a wonderful opportunity: for your art to leave a more lasting mark. It does not require any initial investment (once the work is complete, that is) and does not require restocking or reprinting.

Other Opportunities

There may be other income-generating opportunities in your field. Discovering them requires you to experiment to find out where you feel comfortable. As a freelancer, you'll probably explore avenues that don't feel like a good fit or are uncomfortable—a sign, perhaps, that this path isn't for you. In your experimenting, you can begin to identify the places where you do feel good: Do you like talking to people? Do you feel you have wisdom to share and that you are good at sharing it with others? In this last case, for example, you could offer specialized consulting services. And if you feel you have a story to tell, and are a skilled writer, you might start a blog about design, illustration, or photography. Through experimentation, trial and error, and paying attention to what you enjoy and the feedback you receive from others, you will find your niche. You will see that everything you do begins to intertwine and relate, simply because you are the one who is doing it. This is how your work will begin to make sense, because it is made by you and adapted to your way of being, thinking, and doing. That's what makes it truly unique.

I love teaching. My first step was to start teaching workshops. Later I was encouraged to create online classes in English and Spanish. Over time, I realized that the way I had structured the content was really useful for people, so I thought I'd go a step further and write books that expand on that structure. The first one I published based on my online lettering classes was entitled The Golden Secrets of Lettering. This book you're reading right now is also the result of a successful online class about freelancing.

Now it's time to define what you want to do and what network you want to use to do it. You want to start selling your own products and you have a cousin who has an e-commerce platform? Connect with her and ask her guidance in starting your own online shop. Do you want to teach online classes? Is there someone you know who can lend you a camera and equipment to film it?

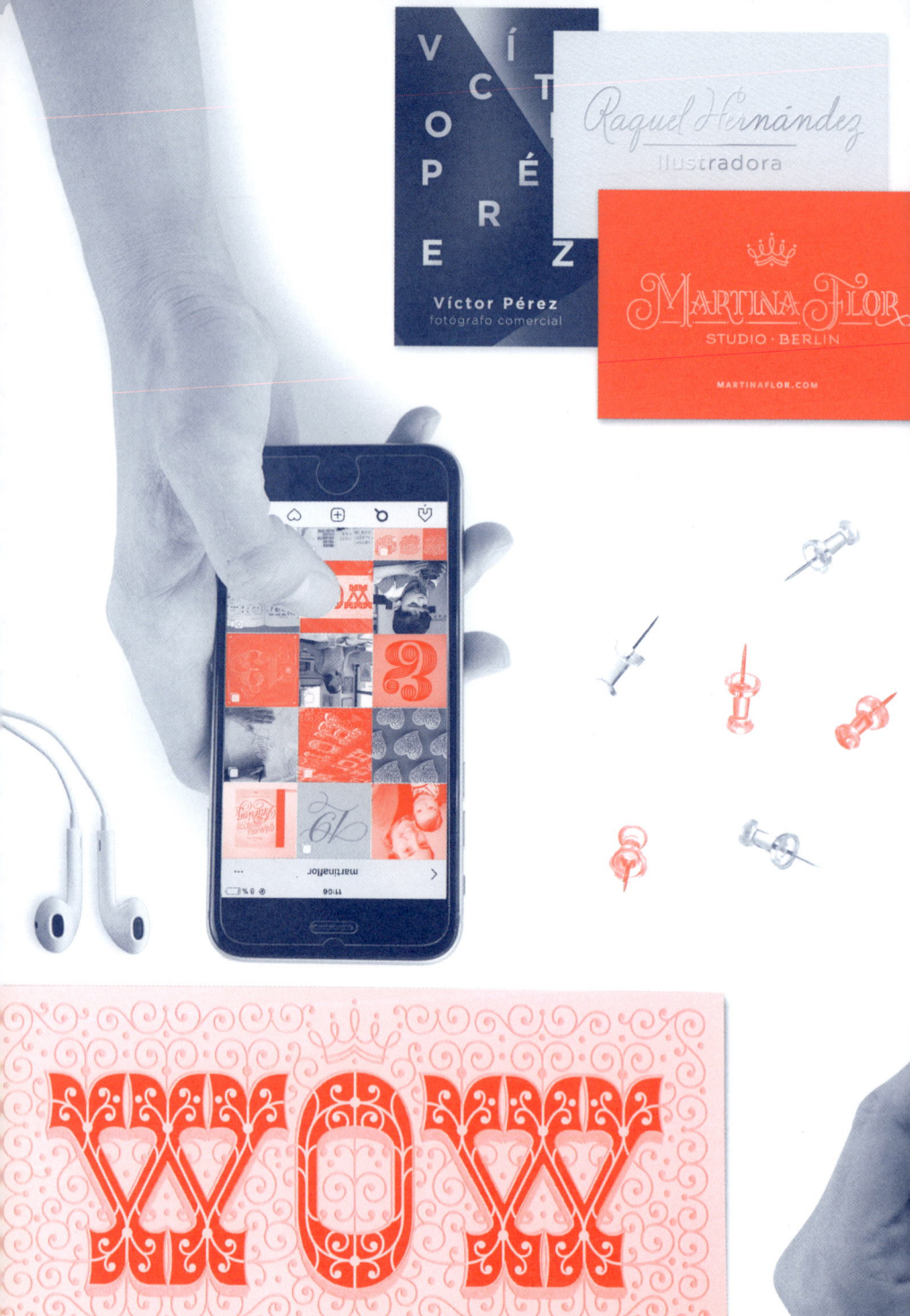

4. Finding Clients

It's time to go after customers and explore where to find them. We will also look at the pros and cons of working with an agent as well as how to build an audience on social media networks, discussing each platform in detail.

Where and How to Find Clients

As I noted earlier, the attitude of the freelancer should be that of an entrepreneur. You have to go out there and find what you are looking for. Above all, you have to tell the world what you're doing and that you want to get hired. Actively looking for jobs is the necessary first step that will lead to clients seeking you out. Let's go through your options for finding clients from least challenging to most.

Your Personal Network

The first thing is to tell your network of friends, acquaintances, and relatives that you're now self-employed, outline what you specialize in, and make yourself available. Members of your personal network will be the first to recommend you for a job and spread the word about your availability even if you have not worked for them directly. If your friend hears that her colleague is looking for a graphic designer or a photographer, for example, she might remember your e-mail and pass along your name. Additionally, if she needs something done in your field, you will be her first point of reference. If you've done work for her for free in the past, this will also be the signal that this is now, officially, your job, and will be done during paid working hours.

Social Media Networks

It is difficult to know with certainty whether having accounts on social media networks makes it easier for you to get commissions or not; it depends a lot on the type of work you do and how you use the platforms. However, social media networks are a good way to stay in touch with colleagues and clients you already have, and keep them updated on your activities and the projects you're working on. Later in this chapter, we will look in detail at the potential of each social media network. As a general rule, it's best to try each out yourself to see if it works for you and benefits your business, or else becomes a drain on your time and energy.

Coworking

Coworking spaces are a good alternative to working from home, because instead of working all by yourself, you will share a space with other professionals and freelancers. While we will address the benefits and downsides of coworking spaces in more detail in the next chapter, it's important to point out here that they can be great places to meet others in your field, or in complementary fields. Over time, you can build connections and develop professional relationships with others in the space. This can present numerous opportunities, such as the possibility of collaborating on projects. Or say a graphic designer in your coworking space is doing a campaign for a client and needs illustrations—they might give you the assignment, not only because you'll do a fabulous job, but also because you are the closest and most accessible person. Sharing workspace invites the opportunity for teaming up with others if a larger assignment comes in.

Events and Conferences

Seeking out potential clients and customers at events and conferences can be slightly nerve-racking but it's a great idea! Look for conferences, seminars, and festivals that bring together professionals from your field or the fields that you are interested in working in. Some events are free and specifically designed to connect you with others and encourage community between entrepreneurs.

CreativeMornings, for example, is a breakfast that is open to the public, free of charge, and offered in cities around the world. At these events, a creative specialist/expert (e.g., designer, entrepreneur, consultant, photographer) gives a brief talk on a specific topic. Attendees are invited to stick around and connect afterward over coffee. These events can inspire new ideas and give you the chance to make professional connections as well as meet potential clients.

However, it's not always easy to start a conversation with someone you've never met. But here's the key to CreativeMornings or similar gatherings: the expert's talk gives you a perfect starting point for conversation. You can open with something as simple as, "What did you think of the talk?" This could lead to a conversation about what this stranger does and what their specialty is, and might give you room to introduce yourself, share what you do, and suggest exchanging business cards. Without realizing it, you will have created a connection with a potential colleague.

I used to attend the TYPO Berlin conference every year. I made many friends and connections there. Through engaging in conversation with strangers, I met the editor of my first book, The Golden Secrets of Lettering.

Public Speaking

Speaking engagements position you in front of others in your field, and that's a position you want to be in as a professional. While your goal might be to speak at conferences and events, it may take some time to get to that point if you are just beginning. But it's a very worthy goal, as speaking in front of an audience can connect you with potential clients. After one of my first talks I was approached by an editor who later became one of my main clients. We had a two-minute talk, he handed over his card, and after a meeting he assigned me a project.

It's true that conference organizers generally look for individuals with a lot of experience and a solid audience. There are, however, conferences that invite talk proposals, which are then reviewed by a jury that selects which presentations will become part of the official program. If public speaking is something you are interested in doing, this is a good way to start. If you manage to have your proposal accepted and are invited to present it, this may lead to other invitations to conferences. This way the wheels start to spin.

It is best to propose a talk about a very specific topic, or else your own stories of success and/or failure. Avoid extremely wide topics, such as "graphic design and art deco" or "postwar photography." Go for something closer to home, such as a personal experience or a process you love.

I regularly print postcards, which I take to conferences or use to send messages, and every year I create a greeting card that I send to clients and friends. In my early days as a freelancer I made an interesting promotional piece. My budget was limited, and I decided to print a poster in one color. The copy read "This will be a fantastic year," in German because at the time I was living in Berlin and wanted to reach local customers.

Even today, when I visit studios in Germany or the homes of colleagues, I sometimes find the poster hanging on the wall. The message resonated with many people—many took pictures of it and posted it to their social media networks, making my work visible to many others.

Promotional Material

Promotional material and merchandising are effective tools for making an impression on potential customers. Once, when I gave my card to the manager of a major design company in Berlin (it was printed letterpress in two colors on a thick, textured paper), he took it and, feeling the texture of the paper, told me that in his youth he used to collect greeting cards. We talked about letterpress and he even recommended some printers in Berlin. I made an impression on him. Through that promotional piece, merely because of the paper it was printed on, I evoked memories, triggered emotions, and started a conversation. I have retained that client to this day.

By distributing a promotional product, you are putting a piece of yourself on someone's desk. Products that take the form of postcards, business cards, posters, or 3-D objects are an excellent way to showcase your work and ideas. A promotional item doesn't necessarily have to be sophisticated and expensive—it simply has to reflect the quality of your work. Producing promotional material is something that should become a regular task.

Circulating your business name and your work, no matter the format or the means by which you do it, is essential to growing professionally, and distributing promotional materials is a good way to do it. It is, however, not the only way, as we will see later.

Cold Calling and E-mailing

Personally, I'm not a fan of receiving unexpected phone calls, and even less of a fan of those that take more than a few minutes. However, a call can optimize your other attempts to open doors to a potential client or collaborator.

For instance, you can make a brief call to find out the name and business e-mail of the creative director of an agency or the editor of a publishing house. You can then send your promotional material, or a personalized e-mail, to the head of the relevant department. That way your contact information won't pile up among other random correspondence at the reception desk, or get lost among the other e-mails directed to info@xyz.com. Here is a template for a brief cold call: "Hello, my name is Alex, and I've wanted to work with you for a long time. My expertise is in landscape and portrait illustration. I would love to bring my portfolio to you, or send you an e-mail with a link to my website. Would that be all right?"

Ideally, the response on the other end of the phone will be, "Yes, of course!" Most people are friendly and most companies are looking for new talent. Follow up (and quickly!) with what you have agreed to by phone. You can always send an e-mail instead of cold calling, but you risk not receiving an answer, and the likelihood that your message will end up in a spam folder is pretty high. A brief phone call has the power to create some sort of personal commitment.

Other Ways to Reach Customers

There are infinite ways of approaching potential clients. In short, it's about dealing with people, and in this, you need to understand what you are best at. If you are great at making conversation, sign up for events where you can have a chat and connect with peers and clients in person. Do you enjoy staying in the studio thinking up creative pieces that will surprise and draw attention? Go ahead, surprise us. Are you into guerrilla design? Good, go out and wallpaper the city.

The important thing here is to go out and look for opportunities, and not wait for them to come to you. The former depends on you, and the latter is, to a degree, out of your control. In the first case you are in power, in the second you are not. Get ready to take control of what happens to you.

Working with an Agent

As a freelancer you have the option of working with an agent, especially if you are an illustrator, photographer, or animator. The agent is someone who represents you and serves as an intermediary between you and your future clients. An agent will negotiate your fee and take care of the whole administrative process, such as negotiating and signing contracts, invoicing clients, and intervening in any conflicts that arise during the payment process. For this reason, the agent or representative receives a percentage of your profit, ranging from 20 to 50 percent, depending on the work, the agent, and the client. Working with an agent is not for everyone. However, the specifics that an agent manages can be stressful and take up a lot of time, and having an intermediary can save you a lot of headaches.

Advantages

A representative, as long as they do their job well, can be a very powerful ally. An agent can connect you with great clients. Corporate clients, for instance, rarely contact freelancers directly, and they like to negotiate contracts and budgets with someone experienced in that process. This is where the agent plays a fundamental role, not only in facilitating the hiring process, but in ensuring you are fairly compensated for your efforts and your time in executing the assignment, as well as protecting your rights. If one of your goals is to work with large brands that have national or international exposure, having an agent will probably improve your chances of doing so. This does not mean that you can't accomplish this goal without one.

Your agent is also responsible for promoting your work. A typical modus operandi of a representative is to arrange meetings with agencies, brands, publishing houses, and potential clients to present and promote your work. If you're just starting out, this can help raise your profile, open doors that might be harder to open on your own, and get you the projects you need from high-profile clients to help you build a more solid portfolio.

An agent can also be useful for negotiating higher fees. Since they are an external party, they are not emotionally involved with the project, which helps during the negotiation process. They know the value of certain jobs and are trained to set proper parameters and fees for specific assignments.

In addition, their profit is a percentage of yours, so they will try to negotiate the total fee as high as possible. Negotiating fees and contracts is time-consuming, and negotiations may generate some friction. After a somewhat tough negotiation with a client, moving on to the creative part can be a difficult transition. Having a representative negotiate the fees for you can save you time and shield you from uncomfortable moments, freeing you up to do what you do best—create!

Finally, an agent can raise a client's perception of you by putting you in the "rock star" position: "Julia is too busy creating art and doesn't have time to talk about money." *Touché!*

Challenges

Yes, one of the cons is that the rep gets a percentage of your total fee. As we saw earlier, this is the agent's compensation for taking care of a certain part of the negotiation process as well as other administrative tasks. If you feel confident and able to carry out all of the tasks associated with a project by yourself, you will receive the total fee.

Over time, you will be able to tell if your relationship with your agent is constructive or not. Of course, there's also an initial contract with the agent that sets out the terms and conditions of your working relationship, and you'll need to pay attention to the commitments you'll be making.

Since the agent will be speaking to potential clients on your behalf, it is important that you make an informed decision about who will be representing you. Read your contract carefully and ask colleagues about their experience working with their agents. Have a personal interview with your representative or agency, and learn about how they speak and communicate through social media networks, by e-mail, and on their website. Your agent will become your face to potential clients, so it is important that you and your agent share certain values and ways of interacting with others and doing business. Here, as a general rule, my advice would be: work with people you like.

Types of Contracts

There are several ways to sign with an agent. There are agencies that offer an exclusivity deal, which means that all your clients will be negotiated by your agent, whether they engaged the client or the client reached out to you directly. In this type of agreement, they receive a percentage of all the work you do no matter what and you will not be able to negotiate with clients on your own.

There are also nonexclusive contracts where you are free to have your own clients and collaborate with the agent for certain projects. Clients that book you through your agent go through your agent—your contract for the work is negotiated by your rep. Clients may also approach you directly, and you can choose to manage them on your own. You can negotiate fees and contracts yourself without the agent's intervention, or you can, if you so choose, invite your agent into the negotiation process.

The income share with an agent also varies. There are agents who take a fixed percentage, regardless of the nature of the project. Others charge different fees according to whether the project is, for example, an advertising campaign or an editorial piece. This is directly related to the average budgets available in each branch of the industry. In nonexclusive contracts, agents will usually receive a lower percentage if the client is provided by the represented.

Since you're in charge of the creative work, the copyright always belongs to you. Although it may seem obvious, there are agencies that may limit the right of the artist or designer to showcase the results of projects done through the agency in their personal portfolio once the relationship ends. This means that if you ever decide to end that collaboration, you won't be able to showcase any of the projects you did through that agency, even though you were the author. These kinds of abusive clauses exist and you should keep your eye out for them when signing with an agent.

Finding an Agent

Some methods of reaching out to an agent are more effective than others. Agents receive dozens of cold e-mails a day from professionals that, like you, are looking for this kind of collaboration. If you try to contact an agent this way, your e-mail will likely end up in the trash.

As with clients, focus on those agents you really want to work with—make a short list of your favorites and start there. Put in effort to think about how you'd like to contact them. Nowadays, agencies have their portfolios of artists online and on social media networks, where you can get an idea of the kinds of artists they work with or that they might be looking for. Make sure they don't represent an artist that is doing work that is comparable to yours, as they won't want to collaborate with someone who competes with one of their artists.

When I started out as a lettering artist, I was determined to get a representative. I did research and selected agencies that had a solid portfolio of artists, where my work would be in good company and would stand out. I was in search of agencies that were lacking in lettering artists, or that had artists with a considerably different profile from mine. Then I made a short list of those that I really liked, and from these I chose my favorite and sent them a greeting card. The card was designed and illustrated by me. Each card had three blanks to add wishes for the upcoming year—which I filled in myself:
 1. To be happy.
 2. To travel the world.
 3. To be represented by you.
A week later, I received an e-mail from an agency to set up a meeting, and since then they have been my reps. That simple but bold card caught their attention and initiated a working collaboration.

Look for creative ways to contact them, including face-to-face opportunities. Art and illustration fairs are good places to meet agents. Bring a portfolio with a selection of your best work with you. Remember that agents are very busy people with little time, so choose stunning pieces that show, in one glance, what you are capable of.

Finally, make use of your network. Tell your friends and colleagues that you're interested in finding an agent. You never know who might give you that precious piece of information that opens the door you want to walk through.

Building a Social Media Following

In the past, children often inherited something very important from their parents: their profession. It was once more common than rare that the child would continue the family tradition of being a doctor, electrician, or locksmith, for instance. Family businesses were a reflection of this: generations assuring the continuity of a company.

Along with the company they inherited a network of friends, colleagues, and customers, which allowed the business to continue. In the past, someone born into a family of shoemakers who dreamed of being a different kind of artist might have had to fight against his destiny to actually achieve his dream. On top of that, there might have been no one within reach to teach him a new trade and no network on which to advertise his services. Of course, the possibility of building this social network was there, but the tools to do so were limited.

Today a world of possibilities lies before us. The internet gives us the power to build our social media networks, and to do so with people and potential clients from near and far. Through the convenience and far-reaching magic of the Web, a freelancer working in a creative field can successfully make her own way, create connections with peers from whom she can learn and be inspired, and share her work easily with potential clients. Our geographical location is no longer relevant and we have the freedom to work for clients all over the world. Being self-employed has never been better!

The social media networks that facilitate this come in all shapes and colors, and we can choose the ones we like best. Of course, digital networking requires some work on your part and, like any social network (even the most basic of all: your family), your online networks will need attention and care. Here, we will explore each platform in detail and discover how to master them.

Your Website

Having your own website can come in handy in a lot of different ways. It allows you to document what you are doing and serves as a record of how your work is developing. Often, when I receive a client assignment, I look at my website first to remind myself what projects I've done recently. If there is an element I notice, a style or color palette that repeats, I can get ideas about how I might vary it, or avoid it, in my future projects. An online portfolio (or website) is useful for potential clients and collaborators, as it showcases what kind of work you are capable of doing and reveals the person behind the work.

Now, how do these clients and collaborators reach your website? That's where social media networks can play a major role. It's much less common for someone to find your site through an internet search, and much more likely that they will find it through a social media network.

Instagram

This is currently the ultimate social media network for people working in visual disciplines, because image here is paramount. Instagram is an excellent tool to present your work differently than how you show it on your website or online portfolio.

On Instagram, all the miscellaneous material that didn't make it into your portfolio can shine! It's also a good place to keep followers apprised of your work and involved in what you're up to. For instance, if you are teaching a workshop or hosting an open studio, let people know through your feed. If you have updated your website or there is new content on your blog that is worth reading, share it with your followers. You published a book? Go ahead, shout out!

Don't forget that each image you post creates an impression. If you post several images in a row about your book or new prints and products, or that include your kiddos, a new visitor might get the wrong idea of what you're up to creatively and professionally, and who you are. In other words, keep your feed varied and diverse.

Twitter

Twitter is primarily used to stay up-to-date and to hang out with peers in your community. Tweets can include text, images, links, and animations. Twitter can be a lively platform, and discussion and exchanges often happen quickly and in real time. I use it as a place to ask questions that are professionally relevant, like "What letterpress printer do you recommend?" or ethical questions like "How do I deal with a client who is requesting too many changes?" In addition, you can find interesting and relevant content on Twitter for your professional development: articles, papers, or links to useful websites.

Twitter is not only a tool to access relevant content and stay up-to-date with what's happening in the world, but it can also provide a daily quota of social interaction. As a freelancer, you might spend a lot of time working on your own, and Twitter offers at least one type of interaction right from your computer.

Facebook

Facebook is a social media network that allows you to have both a personal profile and a professional one. You can build a professional profile designed specifically for clients, and another one for friends and family. The power of Facebook, however, is its ability to integrate everything.

Earlier I mentioned that your personal circle—your friends, family, and acquaintances—can become your first source for professional commissions. Facebook makes it super easy for them to find out about your business as well as what's happening

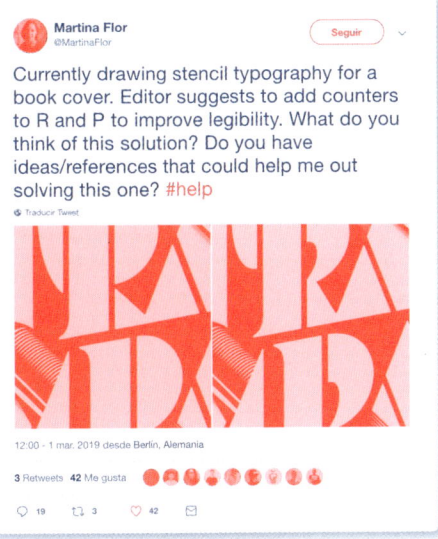

Twitter often helps me find answers to questions, and sometimes helps with solving a specific client-related issue.

Think of Instagram as a sort of light portfolio, where you show the things you are working on and how you are creating them. People love time-lapse videos of artists drawing, showing how they got from the blank page to the final product. They also love personal touches: photos of your studio space, images of things you find interesting or inspiring that feed your creative life, and even personal images. Don't be afraid to let your followers get to know the person behind the account.

Quick tip: Get client approval before you share the process of a commercial assignment, as you might be breaking a confidentiality agreement.

in your life on a personal level. This makes a lot of sense: your work is now a reflection of yourself, what you love, and what you want to do. A picture of your children or of your last vacation might be intermingled with an image from a recent project of which you are proud. You can choose profile and page settings so that only your personal network sees your personal profile, and your clients and potential clients see only your professional profile and not your private one. By creating a separate professional page for your studio or business, you can create work-oriented posts and control how your clients see you and your work.

Behance and Domestika

These are sites or platforms where you can easily build an online portfolio. It's necessary to treat these platforms in the same way as your portfolio on your own site, keeping the content updated with fresh projects. The advantage is that these types of platforms get a lot of traffic and creatives and art directors visit these sites specifically to look for talent. Feel free to document parts of your creative process as these visitors are generally very interested in how you get the work done. These sites also provide the advantage of an inbox where you can receive messages. Since clients will likely contact you directly through this platform, make sure to check your inbox daily.

LinkedIn

LinkedIn is basically a directory of professional contacts that makes you easily discoverable and allows for clients to assess your professional background. For those who work in visual disciplines, it comes up a bit short. You can use it to keep in touch with clients and collaborators without having to add them as friends on Facebook. Remember to add your clients once you are done with their assignments, because they can also provide reviews of your work.

Newsletter

Depending on what you do, newsletters might turn out to be more or less effective.

If you are a freelancer that offers services, a newsletter can help you keep your clients updated about upcoming teaching gigs, online classes, new projects and products, and general goings-on like if you've moved studios. It can also be a nice way to say "hello" and create community with those who follow you.

I don't know about you, but I get a lot of newsletters and know I'll never get to all of them. I often delete all but my favorites. Less might be more in terms of length and of content. The more your newsletter manages to surprise and engage the reader, the more effective it will be. Make sure to add each new client to your newsletter mailing list, and only send announcements when you have relevant news and projects to share.

If you sell goods or products, the newsletter can be a much more useful tool in terms of marketing. Collect contacts through a form on your site or through your online store, as those subscribers are people who are interested in what you do and are interested in your products. If they sign up for your newsletter, they are less likely to be bothered if they receive messages often. They don't want to miss an opportunity to see your newest product or project.

Expanding Your Network

It seems to be a perennial question: How do you get more followers? Think of social media networks as clubs: the more you contribute to the community, the more recognition you receive (which translates into the number of likes, retweets, and followers you get). If you share interesting content, the members of that club will talk about you, and when they share or repost your content they will be "promoting" you. If you lend a hand or give an answer to those who ask for one, you will make new friends that will likely be willing to do the same for you. Social media networks are a virtual reflection of how relationships work in real life.

WOW | We finished our 2018 wowing some friends and collaborators with this laser engraved and hand stamped postcard.

I like sending newsletters twice a year, in which I update my clients and subscribers about recent projects and news. It's hard to believe, but not everyone has an Instagram account and not everyone is on Facebook—a newsletter can be a great (and fun) way to stay in touch.

Instead of focusing on finding tricks and strategies to collect followers, relax and show yourself as you are; be kind and contribute to those little bonds formed on social media networks. Additionally, think of your social media accounts as part of your corporate identity. Try to achieve consistency on a visual level. This includes your profile picture, your cover image, and your handle or nickname. If these are the same across platforms it will make it easier for members of one community to find you on another one.

Creating content for social media networks can take a lot of work, and if you don't keep an eye on it, it can absorb a good percentage of your day. Your focus should be on the work you're doing and sharing online, and not on creating something "shareable." There are ways to ease the process of sharing what you're working on, so that you don't spend so much time on that part. You can, for example, generate content for social media networks each time you finish a client job, and leave all those images or snippets in a folder ready to be shared. There are also applications that can help you manage all your social media networks more effectively, like Buffer or Hootsuite, among many others—apps that allow you to schedule posts ahead of time, and will send you notifications when it's time to share or will share your posts automatically.

Bottom line, creating good work is paramount. If you don't have good work to show, social media networks are useless. We want to be successful creatives and use social media networks as a means to reach a wider audience with whom to share our great work. Don't let these platforms totally absorb you, and assign them the right amount of time: no more, no less.

Put your name out there! Use this sheet to make a list of all the events in (and outside) your city that you'd like to attend in order to connect with potential clients and peers. Take some time to come up with a concept for a promotional piece that helps communicate what you do that you can easily hand to people or send via snail mail. Sketch your first ideas.

5. Day-to-Day Administration

Where you work, how you organize your projects, and how you manage your finances are some of the topics we'll cover in this chapter. We'll also talk about how to create an agenda that boosts your productivity.

Workspace

Although as a freelancer you can work from wherever you want, your workspace might be more important than you think, since you will spend so much of your time there. That said, if you love being in a cafe and feel you can focus properly there, then by all means, enjoy it as your workspace. If you prefer having your own space, adding your personal touch, or spreading out all the materials you'll need on any given day, I recommend looking for or creating a workspace that allows for this. It's essential that you feel comfortable and that your space makes it as easy as possible to perform all the tasks your job requires.

Home Office

As a freelancer, provided your discipline allows for it, you have the ultimate freedom: you can technically work from anywhere. You can work from an Airbnb in Mallorca, from a hotel room in Paris, or at a house-sitting gig in the Berkshires. When you are first starting out, however, you will likely have a long to-do list as well as expenses to pay. Deciding to work from home, at least at first, means you can take "find a workspace" off your list.

For some, working from home means being able to take care of a newborn child or saving time by skipping a commute. No matter what your household responsibilities are (or aren't), maintaining a work life from home will require discipline. It will mean creating and sticking to time slots where you effectively get work done—your home duties shouldn't eat up your productive time. If you're not careful, you might find yourself doing laundry or cleaning the kitchen floor when you're supposed to be working.

If possible, set up a space or room exclusively for working instead of, for example, working on your laptop in the kitchen, reading e-mails on the sofa, and drafting illustrations on the dining room table. Designating a work area or office is both convenient as well as psychologically helpful. When you enter into your work area, you enter into work mode. You have a schedule for the day and you stick to it. You spend solid, uninterrupted time getting things done. Scheduling in breaks, however, including leaving the house at some point during the workday, is as important as sticking to your work schedule.

Coworking Space

As mentioned earlier, a coworking space is basically a large office shared with other freelancers, entrepreneurs, and small business owners like you. If you like interacting with others and would prefer to not spend all day alone, this might be a good option for you. Conversely, if you aren't a very sociable person, and prefer to control your environment—including sound, temperature, and other distractions—you will be doomed in a coworking space.

Coworking spaces are usually set up and designed for freelancers, and facilitate exchanges between them. In addition to offering workstations, these spaces typically offer organized events, talks, and workshops that enable you to exchange and expand your network of peers. Coworking spaces offer various workspace solutions, from renting a table per day to having your own permanent spot. The good thing about working among other freelancers and small business owners is the chance to share experiences, ask for advice (e.g., if you have doubts about an estimate for a job or need guidance on how to deal with a client-related issue), and even get together and set up a team to carry out a bigger project.

An example: If a project you are working on requires photography, it is possible that there will be a photographer in your coworking space with whom you can collaborate. And vice versa: if someone is working on a project that requires your specialty and skill, you'll be at the front of the line. Coworking spaces tend to have a high influx of new members, so you will always have someone new to interact and possibly collaborate with. That said, you must be willing to deal with this turnover, which brings in new people and sometimes new distractions.

Shared Office

An alternative to a co-working space is to start or join a shared office. In this case, you will also work alongside other freelancers, but the crew will be more stable. You will also have a fixed workspace that you can shape to your preference, a true office, but without the isolation that working from home can sometimes bring.

In a community like this, everyone is involved and responsibilities are shared. All decisions are made jointly, from which coffee maker you'll get to what color the bathroom towels are. If something breaks, you may be in charge of repairing it or arranging for repair, and if something needs to be done in the space, you will have to invest time in group meetings and decision making.

Because the turnover of people is much lower, the opportunities to generate connections and working relationships are even greater than in a co-working space. It works very much like sharing an apartment: as a group, you will want to be choosy about who joins your shared space. Similarly, you personally might have the opportunity to propose or recommend new members to the community. Collectively, you can tailor the group so that the office environment meets everyone's needs. Keep in mind that in shared offices there is always a little office management work to do in addition to your freelance work.

Renting Your Own Office

Imagine being able to choose the color of the walls, the arrangement of the desks, and the coffee machine you prefer. All the decisions are yours when you have your own office. There is no group decision making and you will not have to find middle ground with anyone to do this or that thing. If you want to have a meeting, you can. If you want to listen to music, turn it up! It's all up to you!

Having your own office creates a world of possibilities. You will be able to organize spontaneous meetings with clients or collaborators without having to book the meeting room in

When I started freelancing, I worked from home. All I had to do was turn my chair around to go from my office to my bed. I later moved to a community office with other freelancers, but there were fifteen of us, and finding middle ground translated into long debates and a big investment of time.

Today I have my own studio space, which I can shape and use as my business requires. Another plus: I can organize client meetings, hold workshops, and open my studio to guests whenever I desire and with total freedom.

advance. If you have the space, you can host workshops in your own space without the worry of using someone else's facilities. Finally, and very importantly, your workspace can become a part of your personal branding, visually expressing who you are, and helping you make an impression on collaborators and clients. Not only that, but having your own workspace can have a positive impact on your attitude toward work, on your style of organization, and on how you present yourself to customers.

As when you transition from renting a room in a shared apartment to living on your own, you will have to shape and take care of the space by yourself—all chores are yours, from changing lightbulbs to resupplying toilet paper to taking out the garbage.

Time Off

As a freelancer, you decide how much time off you will take. Because you don't get paid vacation like you would with a salaried job, taking time off has a direct impact on your income. Therefore, you'll need to plan holidays and vacations into your annual schedule and assess the financial impact on your business.

Vacations

If having more time off is one of the reasons you want to be self-employed, you might need to determine up front what the ideal amount of vacation time would be. This will be your medium-term goal.

In order to achieve this goal, you'll need to identify the fluctuation of work over the first few years by observing when the hot periods are—when you tend to get a lot of assignments (or make a lot of sales, depending on what you do) and when demand slows. You can then reduce the impact of your time off on your finances.

The truth is, as a freelancer you will very likely end up having to check your inbox during your time off. Even when you firmly decide not to accept any assignments during your break, you might struggle, as I have, with the idea that if you go completely off-line, opportunities may pass you by—which can add stress to a time that is meant to be about destressing!

Consider distributing your breaks throughout the year. This way, you'll have moments to "recharge" and, when you return, work better and with more focus (we'll talk about overall well-being toward the end of the book). In addition, leaving your clients without your services for short periods is better than disappearing for long periods. If a client needs a brochure, he can probably wait two weeks, but if he has to wait a month and a half instead, he will likely look for someone else. Sometimes, however, we need a good long break—in this case, you can also reach out to your network. We'll talk about this later on in this chapter.

Sick Leave

"I'm sorry to hear that you don't feel well. I'll have to get this project done some other way." This is a dagger straight to the heart for a freelancer in development. Being self-employed, you are your work tool and your main source of income, and getting sick has a direct impact on the success of your ongoing, and possible future, projects.

A designer colleague of mine once told me: "Having a child for a freelancer is like having a new project, a very demanding one." The birth of my first son, Milo, brought me a lot of happiness. It also brought on a lot of insecurities: Will I be able to continue working after the birth? Will my clients disappear? Will I be able to work at the same pace as before? For the first few months after Milo was born, I decided not to take on client assignments. That time without phone calls and stressful deadlines gave me the space to enjoy time with my newborn and to write and design The Golden Secrets of Lettering, my first book. Times where your work routine is changed are not necessarily negative and can also become an opportunity to work on something you've been putting off for a while.

Since you're a human being, and therefore vulnerable to getting sick, have a roster of colleagues to whom you can reach out for help when you can't work. You've got an important deadline in two days and you've landed in bed with a high fever? This is when you need someone to cover for you.

This is one of many reasons why it's important to work in an orderly, clear, and organized way—you can then hand off your work to someone else if necessary and they will have no problem navigating your files, materials, and workflow. We'll see later that working in an orderly manner is also essential for the growth of your business, but for now it will also help you react quickly when an unexpected situation arises.

Parental Leave

Congratulations on your latest creation! As a freelancer, you get to choose how much time off you want and need. As these sorts of leaves are usually more prolonged (several months), they can generate a lot of insecurity about how they will affect your future, and the future of your business.

The good news is that, unlike with your sick days, here you know the details up front, including the all-important deadline: the baby's due date! This means that you can spend a few months planning your leave so that you can spend valuable time with your baby and reduce the impact of the time off. You could, for instance, hire another freelancer in your network, on an hourly basis or per project, to cover for you for a longer period of time, even preparing this person to answer your e-mails and keep your workspace in order.

It is likely that during this period your income will decrease, but your focus must be on finding a good compromise that will allow you the time you need with your new baby while also keeping your business running and your clients happy—you don't want to have to start from scratch when you're back to work.

Managing Your Finances

Having control over the money that is flowing in and out is an essential part of growing your business; I wish someone had told me this from the very beginning. The year I began keeping track of my monthly finances was followed by a year in which I doubled my income. True story. Having control allows you to plan and invest, as well as cut back on unnecessary expenses, keeping tabs on what works and what doesn't.

Keeping accurate and helpful records requires consistency—you need to account for all your income and expenses without exception. You can simply keep one spreadsheet where you record all your income and another where you track your expenses each month. Your income minus your expenses will

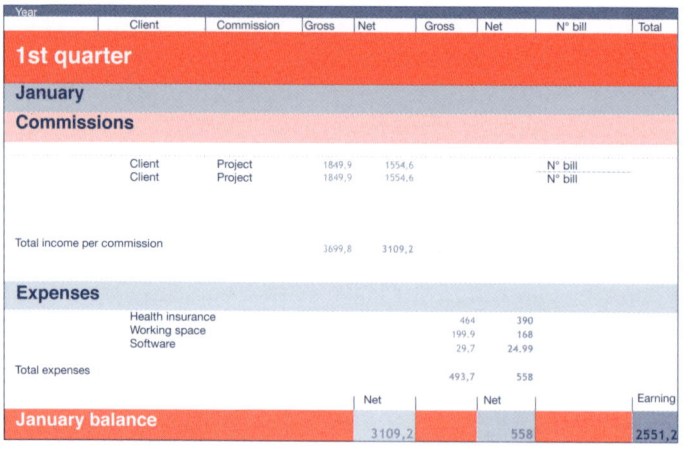

This is a sample sheet for finance management—you can use a spreadsheet program such as Google Sheets, Excel, or Numbers, as well as applications like Expensify, Zoho, Mint, or You Need a Budget). Keeping a consistent, organized financial record gives me a realistic snapshot of how my business is going. When a month doesn't go very well for me according to the numbers, it motivates me to work harder next month and reverse the trend. Furthermore, if you have a surplus, you can consider investments that will help you grow your business.

give you an overview of what is actually going into your pocket—before you pay your taxes, that is, depending on where you live. The tax rate for freelancers typically varies from 20 to 45 percent, depending on a number of personal factors.

Your spreadsheets can be more or less sophisticated depending on your needs. If you do client work and also teach workshops, you can distinguish these income streams by putting them in different categories and see which activity brings in more profit. You can go even deeper, of course, and create subcategories. For instance, within the "teaching workshops" category, you can subcategorize into online classes and face-to-face workshops. All this information will offer you guidelines to fine-tune your operations, get rid of unproductive activities, and optimize your income.

With expenses: you can create a subcategory for recurrent expenses (electricity, subscriptions, workspace), and occasional expenses, such as plane tickets, hardware purchases, and more. This way you can identify which expenses can be cut and which are strictly necessary.

Of course, expenses and income are related, and teaching a workshop (and having associated income with it) will involve occasional expenses (such as paying to rent a space or make copies of handouts). The important thing is, of course, that your overall profit exceeds your expenditures.

Time Management

To be a successful freelancer and have a sustainable career, it is paramount to train yourself in effective time management by developing healthy time-tracking, time-keeping, and planning habits. You will often work on various projects with different clients at the same time, which means your projects will be at different stages that require different tasks.

What is the best way to manage this? We will explore this as well as reveal the keys to organizing an agenda that helps you use your time effectively and boost your productivity.

Using an Agenda

Your agenda will become your best friend and the key to your productivity. And if you learn to make good use of it, you'll see the results quickly. Forget about "to do lists." You need to combine your tasks, estimate time needed to execute them, and then assign those tasks to time slots in your schedule. Just like with finances, having control over your time allows you to be realistic with how much work you can take on each day and how much time a task actually takes to complete.

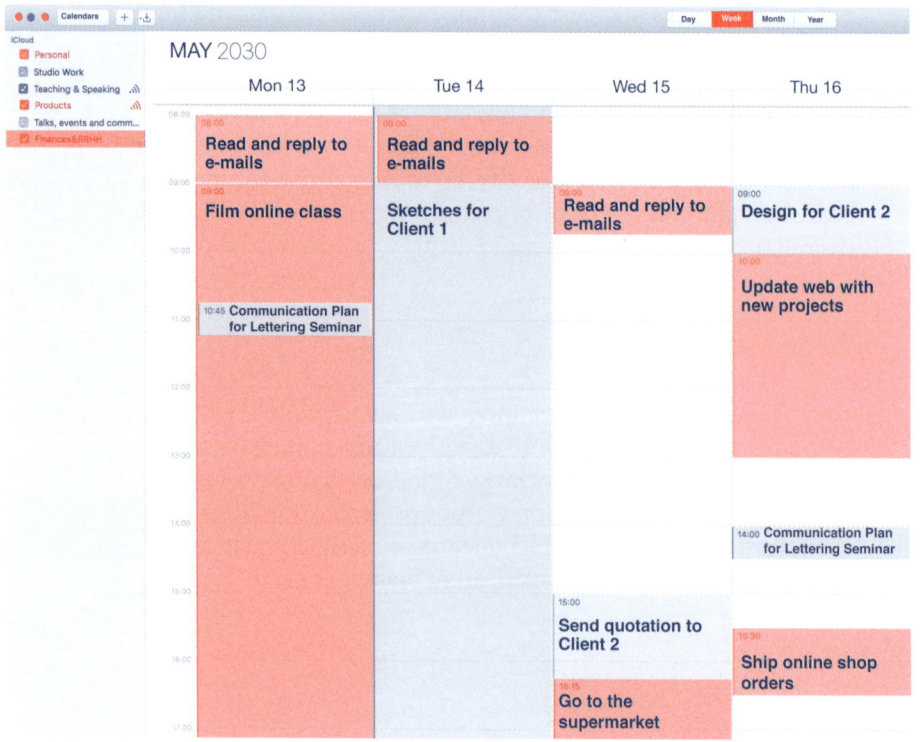

There are many online task management applications (e.g., Todoist, Asana, or Monday, to name a few) and they provide several functions for creating projects, breaking them down into individual tasks with associated deadlines, and even collaborating with teams. If you would like to keep it simple, a calendar will be enough to handle the tasks that you will have. Here are a couple of tips to consider when setting up your agenda:

Color: Organize your tasks by categories and use color to differentiate them. Each color can represent the different areas of your business. For example, you can assign one color for your teaching and another for your client work. You can also assign a color to other tasks, such as administrative duties or studio management.

Time Slots: Whenever you add a task to your agenda, think about how much time you'll need, and be as realistic as possible. This way, each task will be assigned the time and space that it needs, which will allow you to plan, be realistic with client deadlines, and have some control over your time. A tip: Once you estimate how much time a task will take, double it. It's proven (and it's my experience as well) that we tend to be very optimistic about our productivity.

Tasks: Include all your daily tasks on your agenda, not just work tasks. If you have to take your kids to a birthday party at three o'clock in the afternoon, this won't be a good time for a conference call with a client.

Recurrent tasks: Identify your recurring tasks and assign a fixed time slot each week in which you will perform several of them together. That way, you can perform comparable tasks faster. For example, you can assign one day a week for invoicing and bill payments. You can also block out time on a monthly basis to update your website and portfolio.

Organization: Put aside an hour one day a week (I do Mondays) to update your calendar and add new tasks or reassign others. Assigning your tasks to time slots in your calendar is one of your most important and effective work tools, so don't neglect it!

Managing Your Workload

Managing your workload is a challenge you will likely have to deal with on a daily basis throughout your working life. As we've already discussed, the workload of a freelancer fluctuates: after a period without commissions, it's possible that three projects will come in all at once.

Your reasons for accepting an assignment can be varied: maybe it simply pays well, or it's a fun assignment and you feel like doing it, or it will contribute to building your portfolio. Before accepting each assignment, however, you must know for sure that your schedule allows for it. Keeping an organized agenda is one of the things that will allow you to determine whether you have the time to take on new work.

Another factor that can boost your productivity when you're under pressure is to determine procedure for some of your tasks. Keeping an operations manual (the term sounds technical but it's merely a step-by-step description of your workflow and processes) can save you a lot of time. This way when you need to set up your space for teaching a workshop, or when it's time to deliver final files to a client, you won't have to reinvent the wheel. In this same spirit, you can create e-mail templates for e-mailing with your clients, or boilerplate copy for answering questions that you get asked regularly by customers in your online shop. This way, when handling more than one project at a time (which you'll very likely do), you can save tons of time as well as head space. We'll speak about operations manuals and what they could include later on.

When you have assignments that overlap with each other, it can be helpful to set up flexible deadlines (between Monday and Wednesday, for instance) instead of committing to fixed delivery dates. Finally, keep your network of collaborators in mind; you can always reach out to them when you have too much on your plate. It's of course preferable to give up part of your income rather than mess up a project and lose a client.

Learning to Say "No"

Learning to say *no* to clients is a career-long undertaking. In the freelance world, saying no to an opportunity means, necessarily, that it will go to someone else—another dagger directly to the freelancer's heart. The risk of saying yes to every assignment that comes your way—no matter if you want to do it, if it pays well, or if it helps you build your portfolio—is that there may be no time left over for those assignments you really want to say yes to. Saying no, in other words, is also saying yes.

The other risk is that by saying no, you will end up with no projects at all. This is a fear you will learn to manage. Remember that any free time means you can develop other aspects of your business and get new assignments. As a freelancer, time is on your side.

Using Your Free Time

As I mentioned at the beginning of this book, when you're self-employed there's never no work. The success of your business depends on numerous elements that intertwine and make things run smoothly. It's not only about delivering a job on time, but also about presenting it on your website in a way that might attract new assignments. It's not about putting that new product on your online shop, but also about promoting it and making sure customers know about it. It's not only about organizing a workshop, but also about getting registrations. Everything you do has layers of complexity and requires creative time management.

At the beginning of your freelance endeavor, you may find yourself with enough extra time to keep up with maintenance tasks—updating your portfolio and financials—but at some point it may seem like you do not have time to do these things or to think about the future. Treat your project maintenance tasks as if they were for a client, and give them space on your schedule. It's easy to go a whole year, or even half a year, without updating your website just because you "didn't have a free minute" to do so. Don't save these kinds of important tasks for when you have a "window" in your schedule. Remind yourself that they are essential to keeping your business running.

You have completed all your maintenance tasks and you still have free time on your hands? Hallelujah! Take the afternoon off just because as a freelancer, *you can*. Alternatively, you can use that time for creative procrastination and, for instance, lay out that self-initiated project you have been delaying for a while, plan your next exhibition, or brainstorm the concept for your book. Exploring new paths for your work and your business is vital, as is allowing time for creative development, such as learning a different skill or improving on one you already have. Bottom line: transform your free time into creative energy for your business, for experimenting, and for exploration. This can have an immense impact on your work.

Organizing Your Process

In order to organize your process and be able to systematize some of the many tasks you need to perform, it can be very helpful to develop your own instruction manual, or operations manual. Large companies with many employees frequently work with these. They stipulate ideal ways to perform certain tasks, ensuring that no matter who performs them, they can be done correctly by following documented steps. This cuts down on training time for each new employee, and can remove unknowns from the equation for recent hires.

You'll notice that your daily work is full of recurring tasks: answering e-mails inquiring about rates, preparing quotes, updating your portfolio, answering student questions, and more. Having an operations manual when you work on your own will save you time—you won't have to think about what steps you should follow each time you need to perform one of these recurrent tasks. Also, having a documented procedure gives you room to improve that procedure over time, making you more and more efficient at what you do. Your operations manual may include:

Templates you can use when answering common inquiries from potential clients: Boilerplate copy for predetermined e-mails might include an answer to the most common question you receive plus possible questions back to the client so you can better understand the project. If you work in different languages, you can get your answers proofread ahead of time by a professional or native speaker.

Templates to answer frequently asked questions: You may begin to receive e-mails with general questions and collaboration or material requests. Students may write asking about your classes, or potential customers interested in some of your services or products. Instead of investing time in developing a personalized response for each question, you can create an e-mail that redirects the person to links or resources where they can find the information they are looking for.

To-do lists for frequent events: These come in handy and might include what to bring with you when meeting with clients or what to prepare each time you teach a workshop. No more wasting energy in planning what you need each time.

Procedures for recurring tasks: Launching a sale in your shop or updating your portfolio are tasks that will probably repeat. Each one involves a series of steps that you must complete (e.g., optimize photos for uploading to the web). If you have the specifications detailed in your manual, you will know exactly what size and resolution they need to be before you begin.

Information about your business: Having your bank account and PayPal information, usernames for applications, and information about suppliers and collaborators in an easy-to-access place can be a big help.

Administrative procedures: You will likely have to declare your taxes on a regular basis and, whether you have an accountant to help you with that or not, you will have to provide or have accessible the necessary documents and records. Having a list of stipulated tasks that need to be done for filing your taxes will help you deliver the documents correctly.

<u>Technical information:</u> How to install your printer, how to scan in high resolution, or how to connect your tablet to a new computer are tasks that can take several hours if you haven't done them in a while. Having clear instructions handy will help you not to waste time.

It's time to think about where and how you want to work: Where will you set up your workspace? What tasks will you take on during your first few weeks of freelancing? What expenses will you need to attend to more immediately? Regarding your workspace, take note of all the alternatives and their costs, and think of the first goals, or tasks, you want to achieve during your first weeks of work. These might include working on your website, opening accounts on social media networks, or taking photos of your projects. Once you have your final list, add these tasks to a calendar. Finally, list all the expenses you will need to cover during your first three months of self-employment (e.g., website, health insurance, workspace, hardware, and software).

Possible workspaces

Goals for first few weeks as a freelancer

Fixed expenses in the first three months

Variable expenses in the first three months

Martina Flor
STUDIO · BERLIN

Offer Nº. 173204/24

Editorial Fantástica
Something Street - 38 13567 - DF México

Studio Martina Flor
Lettering & Custom Typography

Studio:
Sparrstraße 20

13353 Berlin
Germany
Phone number. +59 000000000
Name: Martina Flor
Bank: German Bank
Account: 010101010101
BIZ: 123456789
IBAN: DE95 9999 0000 5555 7777 00
BIC (Swift): GERTDEDB360

Membership number: 35/446/09845
International tax number: DE00005555

Book cover for *A Drowned Maiden's Hair* by Laura Amy Schlitz

GENERAL CONSIDERATIONS AND RIGHTS OF USE

The general considerations and rights of use are described on the document *Terms and Conditions*. The Copyright and intellectual property belongs to Martina Flor.
If this order is cancelled after the quote is approved, Editorial Fantástica will pay at minimum 50% of the project fee. If it is cancelled after the sketch or proposal is approved, Editorial Fantástica will pay

PROJECT
Book cover.

USE
Printed book cover and promotional materials.

DURATION
Five years.

6. Getting the Job Done, Part I—Securing the Assignment

Here we will prepare you for your first assignment and face what will be one of the most difficult parts of your job: pricing your work. I will guide you step-by-step in how to interact with a potential client in order to close the deal.

Receiving an Inquiry

Attention, an e-mail inquiry has arrived! This is the beginning of a potential assignment and you should try to act as quickly as possible. E-mail inquiries come in infinite shapes and sizes: some include all the necessary information from the start, including a project description and the available budget. When this is the case, your work is simpler, as you will have all the information in hand to accept or reject the assignment. This is a decision you shouldn't take lightly, because accepting an assignment is assuming a commercial and, in many cases, legal commitment to your client. Here are three key questions you should ask yourself before saying yea or nay:

<u>Can I work with the proposed schedule?</u> Confirm that you have the necessary time available to do the job properly and deliver it on time.

<u>Am I interested in the work?</u> Being "interested" in a project can mean different things depending on your circumstances: Will it add to your portfolio? Will it move your work in a different direction? Will it help you pay the bills?

<u>Can I do the job competently?</u> Do you have the professional skills and technical tools to do it successfully? Here, you can refer back to your scope map from chapter 1.

Declining an Assignment

Whatever the decision, always try to answer that first e-mail in less than twenty-four hours. If you decided to decline a job, be sure to thank your prospective client for considering you for that project and briefly explain your reasons for declining. One thing that is always appreciated is your recommending someone else for the job. Remember again that what goes around comes around!

Taking an Assignment

Have you decided to take the commission? Bearing in mind that the client likely had other freelancers to query, take a moment to

thank them for having thought of you for this task. You'll want to clarify all of your questions about the briefing, if any, and list them in your answer. You will confirm your commitment to the client and note any additional information you may need to start working.

Also, you can share a bit about your process, so the client will know what to expect from you as you move forward with the project.

Depending on the type of assignment, the client may be able to provide a contract. Otherwise, you can send an offer according to the available budget, also stipulating your conditions (more on this later). That way, you accept the job and create a legal framework, if not a contract, between you and your client. Once you have drafted your e-mail, don't forget the golden rule in communications with clients: proofread your work! Spelling mistakes make a poor impression.

Finally, there are cases in which inquiries arrive with a quote request (i.e., without a predetermined budget). You will then need to research the client as well as the type of assignment in order to outline a quote that fits the scope of the project.

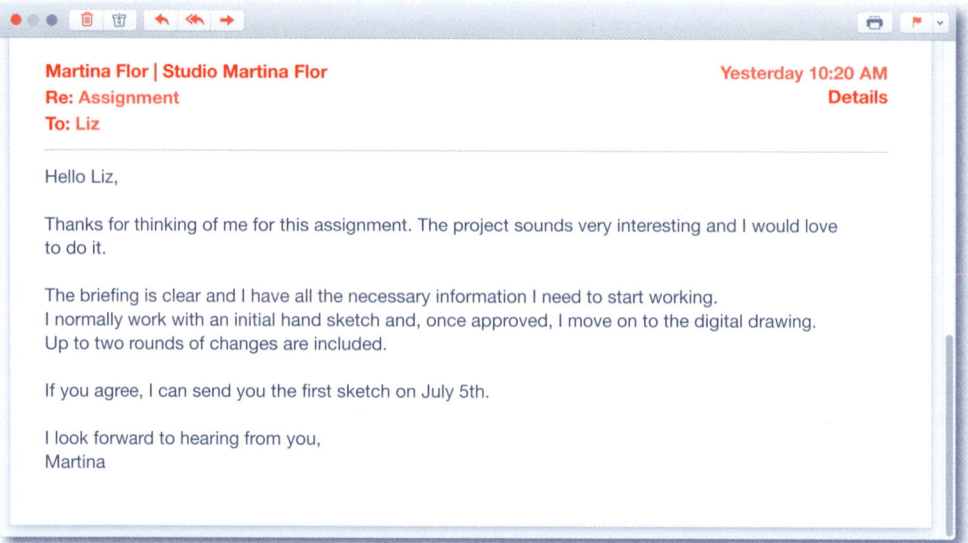

Types of Assignments

Not all assignments pay equally; however, there are certain standards with respect to the type of assignment and its remuneration. This does not mean that there are no exceptions.

Assignments coming from print media outlets, such as magazines and newspapers, are generally associated with small budgets as well as short-term usage rights (usually one year). Here, however, your work will get lots of exposure, and usually the briefing has the potential of generating a good piece for your portfolio. Likewise, publishing houses are usually working with relatively small budgets but give you the opportunity to create a significant piece, like a book cover, for your portfolio.

Assignments that have to do with the identity of a company have variable budgets, which are generally tied to the size of the client. Creating a logo for the bakery next door is different from creating a logo for a national brand that manufactures and markets cell phones. Similarly, developing an interior design concept for an international bank should pay far better than the same job for a local community center. In the first case, the number of times your work will be applied in different contexts will be much greater. Assignments related to the field of advertising generally have bulky budgets, as they tend to involve multiple, high-profile applications. Rolling out an advertising campaign not only involves the creation of the artwork and the graphic pieces themselves, but also booking spaces where those graphics will appear, such as billboards, print media, television shows, and events. The total investment is higher for the client so the available budget for the artwork will be as well.

Product development and packaging also tend to involve large budgets. You'll be contributing to the creation of a piece that is reproduced in bulk so your pay should reflect that. Here, the design itself plays a critical role in the success of the product. Ranges vary according to the market and the country in which a given product will be marketed.

This is a very broad guide to estimating an appropriate rate for a job. We will see in the next section that many factors influence the pricing of your work. For a more detailed breakdown, it's a good idea to look for established fee lists published by unions and professional organizations in your field.

Pricing Your Work

We are about to break into a crucial topic. As a freelancer in a creative field, you will be charging others for something that you love doing. This fact, that you enjoy the work, can get in the way of your ability to assign a sufficient and fair monetary value to your work. The nature of the work can also make it difficult to break it down into smaller parts and calculate the cost of each one of them.

Although an assignment may be to "create a successful design for a brand," or "take a portrait of this client," or "produce an illustration that works with this text," it is important to understand the essential parts of the work process that lead to a successful result. Far from being chaotic, your process has fixed steps—perhaps you always start with a sketch—and requires certain resources, including materials you will need to execute the assignment. Once you identify these things, you'll be able to better understand the value of each part, organize and schedule your work, and assess time and cost on this basis.

When you first start freelancing, the line between charging too little and too much is very fine. If you charge too much, you run the risk of losing the job, and this can feel scary when you're just starting out. Normally, a client will ask for estimates from more than one professional and if your budget is way above average, you'll likely not get that assignment. On the other hand, by low-balling, you risk being underpaid and setting an undesirable precedent with a client, a cycle you want to try and avoid. But fear not. Once you have acquired more experience and have had time to build a reputation, you will likely gain referrals through other clients for whom you've done successful projects, and you can charge fairly for your work. All that said, learning to price your work is a career-long learning experience. Right when you think you have it all figured out, you will find yourself crossing your fingers after sending a bulky quote to a client. Once the client accepts the quote without hesitation, you will think to yourself, "Damn, I should have charged even more!"

Charging by the Hour

It is very common to charge by the hour. One way to calculate your hourly rate is to first determine your day rate: start with your desired monthly income, add that to your monthly expenses, and divide by the number of days you plan to work (twenty, for example). Divide your day rate by the number of hours you plan to work per day to determine your hourly rate. This rate will likely be influenced, or even determined by the specific market you are working in, so it might be helpful to get informed by asking colleagues or checking fee schedules published by relevant trade organizations to find an appropriate figure that works for you.

Whatever rate you come up with can be used to calculate a baseline estimate for a given project. Suppose you receive an inquiry for an illustration. You can estimate how long it will take you, and using your hourly rate, come up with a cost estimate.

You will then add variables onto this fee (more on this later). Although clear and practical, the downside of charging by the hour is that if the project consumes more time than you initially schedule, you will have to renegotiate with the client for that extra time, and this can get in the way of the creative process. It is very likely, however, that through time and experience, you will become faster and more effective. It will take you less time to execute your assignments, therefore you'll charge for fewer hours.

Your speed can be an asset for other reasons. As a general rule, you can charge a 30 to 50 percent "rush fee" for a project that has a tight turnaround time. Calculating a quote for a rush job using your standard hourly fee will ultimately work against you.

In summary: Charging by the hour may be effective at the beginning of your freelance career, but as you gain experience you may want to move toward a cost-per-finished-project model.

Charging on a Project Basis

As you gain experience and proficiency, you will represent a safer bet to your clients. While it may appear cheaper for your client to hire someone whose hourly rate is lower, an inexperienced freelancer poses a risk. If the project is executed poorly, the client will lose time and money trying to make it right.

Hiring an experienced freelancer who charges more can actually be an attractive proposition; the risk that the project will fail is much lower, because the person hired to execute it (that is, you!) is an expert. Since you are experienced, you will know the steps to follow, minimizing trial and error. As a result, you may be able to guarantee a quick turnaround, saving your client time and money.

The client doesn't need to know that you're going to use a vector drawing program for two hours and then hand sketch for three hours, or that you plan to take a day off in the middle of the process. They only need to know that you will deliver their high-quality logo according to the initial brief and in a timely manner. How you get there is not as important (up to a point).

As you gain experience and a reputation, you will be in a position to state your fee without the need to justify each hour you are charging for—when writing up a quote for a project, you'll need only to specify the scope of the project and its complexity. This does not mean that the quote should not stipulate a limit to how many rounds of changes you will accept and a precise number of deliverables. Defining a scope is necessary if you want to execute the assignment successfully.

Types of Customers

There are many variables to consider when pricing your work. The first and most essential from the moment you receive the first e-mail is to understand the size and value of your client, which will allow you to measure the exposure your work will get. Understanding the value of your client's public image will also help you determine how valuable your work will be to them. In other words, a company that has many international branches, and therefore lots of exposure, likely assigns great value to its brand identity. If such a company hires you to design a new catalog (with a print run in the thousands) or to redesign their logo (which will be used in endless communication materials) they are making an enormous investment in their brand identity and reputation, and your compensation should reflect that. The cost of both of these services would be far lower for a local client with only a single branch.

So when an inquiry arrives, research what kind of profile your potential client has, what kind of product they sell, who they work with, what kind of presence they have on various social media networks, and what kind of marketing actions they engage in. Take note of whatever information you can collect. It's relatively easy these days to track what a particular company does and roughly understand its magnitude.

Another important piece of information you should try to find out is whether the client has a predetermined budget for the project. Although they don't always state it explicitly in their first e-mail, a company, whether it is small or large, has an in-house business plan or annual budget that reflects approximately just how much they'll be investing in a certain product or service. To obtain this information, simply ask your potential client, "Is there a budget that I should know of?" You can also be more direct by asking, "How much do you have in mind to spend on this project?"

Knowing this information does not imply that you are not going to put together a higher quote, but it will save you the trouble of preparing a detailed estimate in the event that the client's budget falls well short of what you're willing to do the job for.

Project Details

Once you have analyzed the size and reputation of your potential client, and you know if they have a limited budget, you need to understand the scope of the project. By understanding the magnitude of the project, you can assign a value to each aspect of your work on the project. For example, if your client hires you to create an illustration or a photograph for an advertising campaign with a three-month life cycle that will take over the streets, the subway, and magazine and newspaper stands and appear in online media as well as on TV, it is reasonable to expect that the compensation for your work will be proportional to the total investment in that campaign. In other words, if the company invests a large sum in a campaign where the image you are going to create plays a role, then the work you do for them should be an important part of that investment.

To understand the projects size and impact, here are some questions you should get answers to:

Timing: What are deadlines for the assignment? When should the final product/design be finished? Assess if the due dates your client is proposing are realistic. If they are so tight that you'd have to cancel other assignments in process or hire help, you may have to apply a rush fee.

Complexity: What challenges does the work present? How many pieces do you have to deliver? What else is involved in the process? Taking a portrait photograph in a studio may not be as complicated as a job that requires you to travel to a remote area or attend a certain event out of town. Will you need extra materials? Will the job require special preproduction tasks?

Usage: How long will your image/product be used, and in which regions? Find out for how long your client will earn profit or revenue from what you created. Will your work be used locally, nationally, or internationally?

Exclusivity: This mainly affects those who work with illustration or photography. Does the client want the exclusive right to use your work? Exclusivity means that you will not be able to sell your work to other companies and generate income from it beyond what you earned for the commission. For example, if your client wants exclusive use of a certain photo, you will not be able to sell it on stock photography sites. Sometimes it's worth it to go this route, but in most cases you should try to hold onto the copyright of your work, retaining ownership of your own creations.

Applications: What kind of applications will the image/product you create have? This information will also give you a measure of the overall size of the project and help you assess the scale of the investment that your client is making. If, for example, the client wants to use a photo you have taken in a print catalog, the size of the print run will reflect the scale of their investment (one million catalogs is obviously a much greater investment than one hundred). Again, the fees for your work should be proportional to the total investment of your client.

Once you have all this information figured out, there is only one variable left to consider: your reputation. Your reputation is built through time and through the value of your work.

If you have made a name for yourself by designing logos, the company that comes to you will probably understand that it is paying for your experience, trusts that you have the skills to complete the project, and knows, based on your many successful projects and your great track record, that the risk of things going wrong is very low.

Experience and competence translate into low risk, which is a currency in what you do as a freelancer, and you need to account for it in your pricing. With more time and more successful projects under your belt, your reputation will only grow and improve.

Quotes and Estimates

There are two ways to price a project: You can put together (1) an estimate or (2) a quote. An estimate is, as the word implies, a calculation of what it might cost to execute the entire project, and implies possible additional costs being folded in. If you calculate your fees per hour or charge a day rate, the client will know that if you need to work more hours, you'll charge more. A quote is a fixed-price offer, and means that you are tied to your original quoted fee even if it entails slightly more work than you expected. If you're not quite sure how long a job will take, an estimate could keep you on the safe side. When it comes to quoting, these are the items you should include:

Scope of the Project

As we discussed before, the client does not need to know if you use this or that software to execute the assignment; what is relevant is that the work required is clearly defined, as are the assets you will deliver (and when). This way, you make clear from the beginning that you will be charging for a specific project, no more and no less.

Rounds of Revision

A job can always be done better, and if you don't set clear boundaries, the duration of a project can extend much beyond what is reasonable.
 Restricting the number of rounds of changes and revisions can optimize the process, because it forces the client to take each round seriously and prohibits her from sending infinite batches of additional changes. On the other hand, limiting rounds does not define a fixed number of changes per round, but it does define a stage in the process where you will make a collection of changes all at once.
 Normally, a freelancer will contract for up to two rounds of changes in a design, illustration, or photography process; if a third round is needed, the client will have to pay an additional

cost. Of course, it is up to you to assess whether additional changes beyond what was originally stipulated can be made quickly without incurring additional cost.

Duration

As soon as you accept an assignment, it occupies your schedule for a certain period. If you accept a job that will take you a month to complete, you will have to take into account your professional and personal commitments. Assignments can last from a few weeks to a few months. However, it may happen that your client decides to let the project "sleep" for a year and then wants to resume it later.

Include a clause in your estimate that limits the period during which you are willing to carry out the assignment. This gives you the option to opt out of a project or renegotiate the terms once your client decides to resume work.

Services Not Included

It falls on you to clarify all that is not obvious to those who are not specialists in your area—namely, your clients. Do not leave room for the client to assume you will take care of parts of the process that do not fall into your purview. Say you are a photographer and you send in an estimate for a portrait, which you know does not include retouching or postproduction—you'll need to specify that for the client.

Cancellation Terms

You'll want to include a clause stipulating what happens should the project get cancelled. Accepting a project from a client also implies rejecting others, and knowing that you will be receiving income for a project changes how you are engaging with certain other commitments and investments related to your business (and sometimes your personal life!). As soon as a client cancels an assignment, even if you have not yet executed any phase of the project, there are certain expenses and losses that you will

Offer N°. 173204/24

Offer number

STUDIO · BERLIN

Your name or logo

Editorial Fantástica

Something Street - 38 13567 - DF México

Client and adress

Studio Martina Flor
Lettering & Custom Typography

Studio:
Sparrstraße 20

13353 Berlin
Germany
Phone number. +59 000000000
Name: Martina Flor
Bank: German Bank
Account: 010101010101
BlZ: 123456789
IBAN: DE95 9999 0000 5555 7777 00
BIC (Swift): GERTDEDB360

Membership number: 35/446/09845
International tax number: DE00005555

Official info of your studio

Book cover for *A Drowned Maiden's Hair* by Laura Amy Schlitz

Title of the project

PROJECT
Book cover.
USE
Printed book cover and promotional materials.
DURATION
Five years.
TERRITORY
World.
DETAILS
Costs include image creation with up to two initial sketches/proposals, two change rounds, and vector file.
COST
$4,000

GENERAL CONSIDERATIONS AND RIGHTS OF

The general considerations and rights of
described on the document *Terms and Co*
The Copyright and intellectual property
Martina Flor.
If this order is cancelled after the qu
approved, Editorial Fantástica will pay a
50% of the project fee. If it is cancelled
sketch or proposal is approved, Editoria
will pay 100% of the fee.

incur. Therefore, it is appropriate to establish a basic cost per project cancellation (as a rule, this is 50 percent).

Depending on the discipline you are working in, you can set cancellation costs relative to the stage of the process you are in when the project is cancelled. It is not the same for a project to be cancelled in the concept stage as it is when you are nearing the final stage. Therefore, you can establish one fee for cancellation of the project in early stages and another when it's in its final stages.

Terms and Conditions

Together with the estimate, you'll need to attach your terms and conditions of business, which outlines a set of standards you adhere to. These terms are conceived to protect you and the client in this business transaction. (If you are sending a quote instead of an estimate, your terms and conditions will need to be attached as an extra document.)

They clarify how to handle additional costs that may arise during the development of the project, payment terms, confidentiality, intellectual property provisions, and more. Many unions and institutions make standard terms and conditions of business available to the freelance community. AIGA, the professional association for design, for example, makes documents available for download online.

Sending a Quote

It's time to send the quote to the client and cross your fingers! Sending a quote is, in a way, similar to asking someone on a date. Here are some things to keep in mind during this part of the process.

<u>Clarity:</u> The structure of your quote should be guided by the identity of your studio. Don't forget to clearly and visibly include your contact information, so that the client can reach you easily. Make yourself available to answer questions, and follow up two days after sending your quote.

Approval: If the client approves your quote, keep proof. It can be an e-mail approval, or a hard copy of the quote signed by the client (depending on the country you live in, one or the other will have legal value).

Next steps: Explain to the client how you work. What should they expect after approving the quote? Simply explain the steps you will follow in a few words.

Negotiating an Offer

Your offer reflects the value you place on your work, which means that, if the client wants to negotiate, you will always work from your original estimated or quoted figure. That said, you should know that money is not the only factor in a budget negotiation. If the client cannot afford your fees but you are interested in including their project in your portfolio, then here are some things you can negotiate to make it possible.

Use: You can limit the usage license for that image, photograph, or drawing—the client will have the right to use what you produce for a limited time. And if they want to use it for a longer time, then, at that time, they will have to agree on a new price and make a new contract.

This route gives your client an opportunity to pay for your work as she can afford it. At the same time it allows you to make more for the project in the end, as a license extension implies the success of the product you have made. Here, you must keep track of the expiration of that original license. Once this period has expired, you must contact your client to renegotiate the use.

Trading: If the client makes a product or offers a certain service that may be useful to you, this can become a means of payment. You can negotiate a portion of your fee with an exchange of services or products, in which case both parties come out on top.

The ability to negotiate other variables allows you to maintain the established value of your work. Accepting an assignment for much less than what you initially quoted, without negotiating other variables, threatens your credibility.

If, despite a low offer, you want to accept a job, the client needs to know that you are charging less than usual. You can clarify the real cost in the quote and point out the great discount that you are applying to the project. Upon approval of your quote it's standard procedure that you receive a 50 percent advance. This should be included in your terms and conditions of business.

Licensing

As we saw, the usage license can be an important portion of the total cost for your work or service, because it allows your client to use the product you created and make a profit with it in a certain space (region) and within a certain time period. Of course, a company will always prefer a license for unlimited use, but you can offer a licensing scheme instead (for five or ten years, for instance).

Depending on your discipline, the use of a license will be more or less common. In illustration and photography, for example, a license is a common currency and is always included in cost calculations; in graphic design or in branding, it is less frequent, since, generally, the material produced is suited specifically to the client, and it wouldn't make sense for a client to have to pay a license extension for the use of their own logo.

A license is defined by time, region, and sometimes application. Time stipulates for how long the customer will be entitled to make a profit with your work, and is usually defined in terms of years or else is unlimited (i.e., permanent). The region stipulates a geographical boundary within which your work may be displayed, and is generally delineated by country/countries or else is "worldwide."

Finally, a license can also limit the client's applications or use of your work. A certain illustration will be used only in a catalog, for example, and not in packaging. If the client wants to use your image more extensively and, therefore, make more profit, this should result in greater economic return for you as well. The terms of the license must be detailed in the quote, as these terms are part of the cost calculation. Remember to define a period of time, the region in which your work will be used, and, when relevant, its permitted application.

124 LICENSING

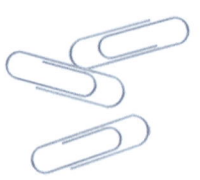

Take a moment to calculate your hourly rate, jot down standard rates outlined by trade organizations relevant to you, note the information you want to include in your quotes, and more.

DONE
is Beautiful

7. Getting the Job Done, Part II—Executing the Assignment

You have succeeded in getting the assignment! In this chapter we will explore how to execute the job in a professional and orderly manner. We will also review the process of invoicing and getting paid.

Executing the Assignment

Your quote was approved—congratulations! Now we will explore how to interpret a client's brief and execute the assignment. Here's an insider's secret: when a client gives you freedom to complete an assignment however you want, this freedom generally turns into a frustrating process with infinite rounds of changes. An experienced client who is familiar with putting together creative briefs will come to you with a clear assignment and a specific idea in mind. This will lead to a more efficient process. If you receive an open-ended briefing, it will be your job to collect as much information as you can about the assignment before you begin.

The client who hired you probably did so because of a project in your portfolio that inspired her. If she gives you an open-ended briefing, you can simply ask if there is a piece in your portfolio that can serve as a point of reference.

Remember that your client is your best ally, and it's vital to get all the clarity you can out of your interactions with her. Your client wants the project to be carried out quickly and successfully as much as you do (if not more!). Be kind and polite during the whole process—your client's input, as a general rule, will help you do your job better.

The Client Brief

Let's look at an example of an ideal brief. Of course, the information included will vary depending on what you do and according to the assignment. However, there are some basic parameters that should always be defined before you start working.

Time frame: When does the client expect to see your proposal? When is the delivery of the final files? The deadlines must allow you to, on the one hand, fulfill your ongoing commitments and, on the other, carry out this new one.

Target audience: Your client knows best what audience they are trying to reach. Having that information will help you home in on how you will approach the project's creative parameters.

Brief

Title: *A Drowned Maiden's Hair,* Author: Laura Amy Schlitz

Genre: historical fiction

Audience: young adults, ages 12+

Format: 6 x 9 paperback

Deadline: final files by July 30th.

Specs: vector layered drawing PDF of full cover spread, 0.125 inches bleed.

Brief: This is a historical novel that takes place in the Victorian era, so we would like the lettering to be inspired by nineteenth-century type design. It should still look contemporary and fresh rather than completely vintage. We would like to use a maximum of three colors.

Back cover: We need space for synopsis and barcode.

Spine: The title, author, and logo of the publisher must appear. Please add decorative elements if you consider them necessary to join spine and cover.

Format: What file format are you expected to deliver? What dimensions should the final artwork be? If these parameters aren't defined by the client, try to get information about what the piece will be used for. Will your creation be sent out via snail mail or e-mail? Are you designing for web, or print, or both? Set up your files with the correct parameters from the outset.

Creative direction: What kind of aesthetic is the client looking for? Is there a point of reference you can use? Here the client should do their best to put into words what they have in mind. They can also provide visual aids.

Keywords: Try to elicit keywords that can help provide direction. These should limit your stylistic palette, helping you pick colors and define other design elements you might work with. Underline guiding keywords in the brief, such as "contemporary," "fresh," "historical," "friendly," etc. With these key concepts in mind you can easily confirm that a certain design or illustration you have made looks "friendly" or "contemporary," for example.

Specs: Depending on the type of assignment you received, limitations may be technical or stylistic. For example, the brief may state that you must work with two colors or that the final artwork must have a specific aspect ratio. This will influence the final result.

Predetermined visual elements: Sometimes a client will provide elements that must be included in our work. If you're designing a book cover, for example, you may need to include the author's name and the publisher's logo. Make sure these elements are provided before you begin work so they do not get left out—they can help you shape and design your piece.

A Professional Work Process

You have a proper brief (either provided by the client or put together through a Q and A process), and now you can start to work. To successfully carry out an assignment, you will need to take responsibility for project management to some degree. This means that you will be active in this working relationship

with your client, not only in executing the work but also in establishing due dates, keeping her abreast of your progress, and requesting feedback prior to revisions.

Organizing Your Process

From the moment you take on an assignment you will be working toward a deadline, or delivery date. All your steps should be geared toward meeting this goal, including allowing time for the customer to review certain milestones along the way to give you feedback.

Part of your job will be to inform the client of what's coming next, with the goal of reducing the number of steps to as few as possible. You will want to keep client e-mails and calls to a minimum, with feedback and revision consolidated in predetermined rounds, so that the client does not get in the habit of sending you many disorganized e-mails, each addressing only a couple of small details.

For many artists, the creative process involves unknowns and can be difficult to predict. When we work for a client, however, we need to protect them from our creative process and the chaos and uncertainty that it sometimes involves. Completing assignments effortlessly (at least, in the eyes of your clients) is part of your job. If your creative process begins with an endless number of sketches, you will want to show your client only a limited selection. It's your job to narrow the options down to what will be most helpful and effective for getting the work done. You want to avoid overwhelming the client—you do not want them drowning in a sea of possibilities.

Identify relevant stages in your work process. For example, if you are an illustrator, you might divide your process into four stages: one in which you present draft ideas, another in which you move forward and polish one of these sketches, another in which you work digitally and add color, and a final stage of digital polishing, after which you deliver the final artwork. By consolidating your work in rounds you can avoid endless e-mails and haphazard feedback.

Staying Organized

Executing an assignment will most likely involve at least a few telephone calls and e-mail exchanges, especially if you count

 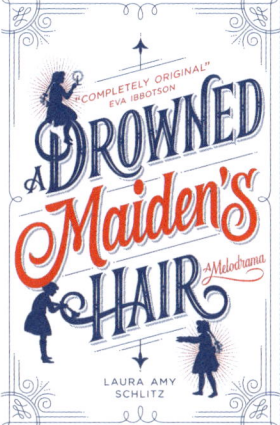 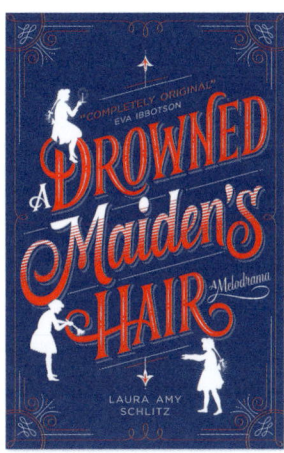

the initial e-mails exchanged during the quotation and briefing stages. If your client is working on behalf of a larger company, your work might also be reviewed by a number of different people who might all have feedback to offer. To avoid the confusion that can result from forwarded e-mails, responses to versions of a file you've already updated, full inboxes, and the like, it's best to keep your project files centralized in one place. That way, everyone who needs to can access your work and get an overview of the initial brief and other important information, such as deadlines and primary contacts.

Creating a private, client-specific page on your website, which only you and your client will access, is one way to manage your workflow and keep a project centralized.

In addition to sketches, drafts, revisions, and final files, this page should contain basic project information:
- The title of the project
- Art director or primary contact
- Project deadlines and delivery dates
- Original brief

By keeping your work organized and centralized you can avoid endless e-mailing and minimize the risk of creating misunderstandings with your client. A centralized page for your project serves as a visible record of your progress, establishing both the starting point and final goal. The client can

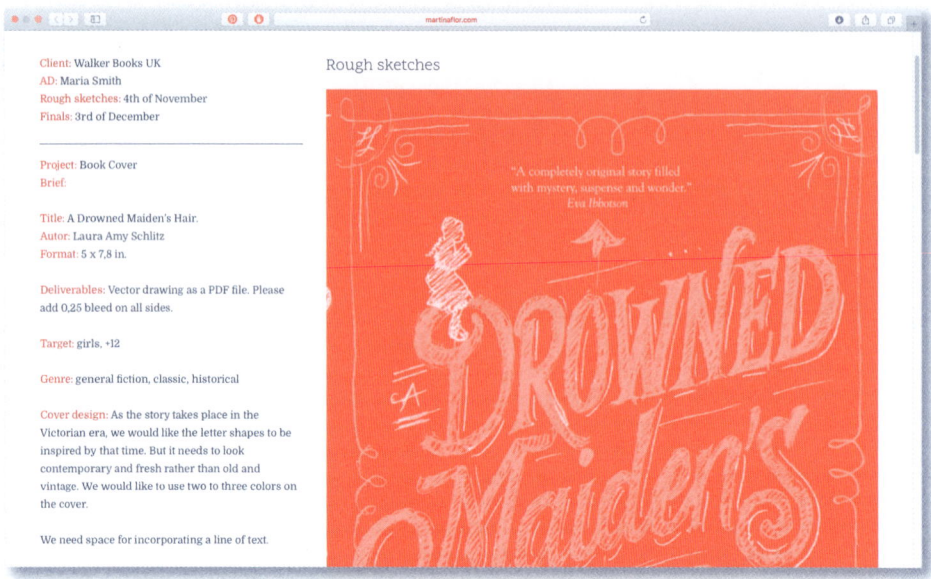

access it to revisit the original brief and remind themselves of important specifics such as how many rounds of revisions are included in the original quote. Having this information available for all to see will make it easier for you to renegotiate terms if necessary. Keep your work labeled with simple and clear headings. Include a downloadable, print-quality version of each revision in case the client needs it for internal meetings. Keeping your work organized in this way serves an important purpose, beyond minimizing misunderstandings: it reveals how much work you have done for your client, and demonstrates the value of it!

Creating a Presentation

Depending on the project and the client, presentations will be more or less elaborate. If you are working on a corporate branding project, you will probably be asked to prepare a multipage presentation that shows the many contexts in which your logo or graphic will appear; if you specialize in product

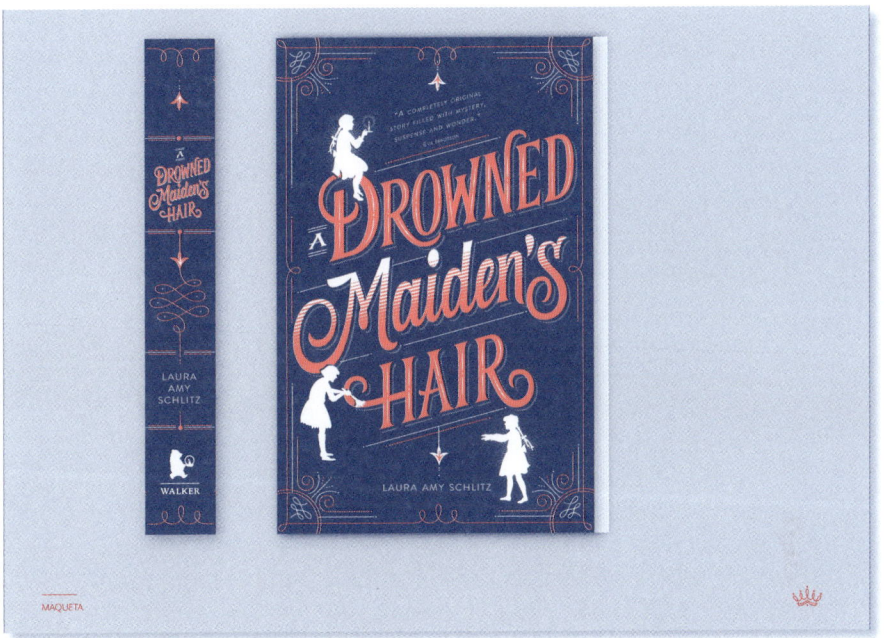

MAQUETA

photography, you might be asked to show several versions of the same photo with and without retouching. It's essential that the client sees only what they need to give feedback on and that your work is presented in a clean and clear way. Here are a few things to keep in mind when preparing a client presentation:

Include the basics: The name of the project and the contact person or creative director at the company should appear.

Keep it simple: Let your designs be the stars of the presentation, and make sure each has space to shine. Don't waste time making decorated presentations and complex animations. Invest your time in making your designs look as polished as possible.

Use your own branding: Include the logo of your studio and your contact info. Keep in mind that your presentation will probably be discussed in internal meetings and shared. Make sure it's clear at all times who created the work.

Include mock-ups: Show your design in a real-use situation. For example, if you are designing a book cover, show a 3-D mock-up of a book with your design applied.

Sharing Your Work

Once you've completed and proofread your presentation—no spelling errors and no missing elements—it's time to share it with the client. Avoid long and complex e-mails; let the work speak for itself. Make sure your message includes the necessary information:
- A brief explanation of what you are sending
- Any link or password that the client must use to access the presentation
- Necessary clarifications

Here you need to trust your gut: Does your client need you to guide him through the presentation? Or is he decisive and capable of assessing your work and providing feedback without additional input? There are clients who will need some guidance and face-to-face exchange in order to move forward. There are others who will be able to assess your work and make decisions based on your presentation alone.

If you feel that your client needs that extra help, make yourself available for a phone call to guide them through the

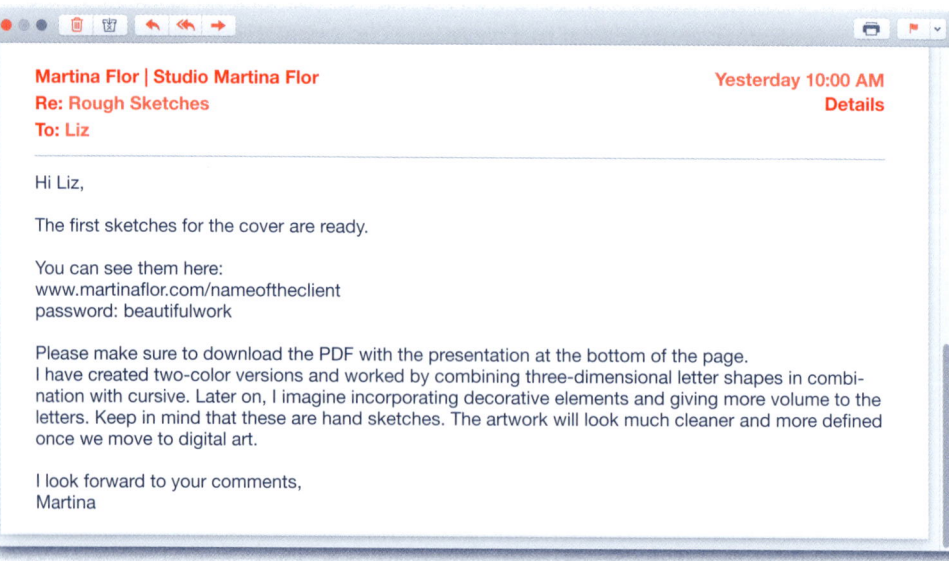

presentation. If the project is big and complex, set up a meeting with the client so you can present your designs yourself. Your presence and management can be the key to the project's success. By the way, don't forget to account for this extra time when preparing your quote.

Receiving Feedback

The company has reviewed your presentation. Now it's time to take in feedback. As mentioned before, customer feedback is necessary because presumably, the client knows the product and the audience better than you do.

As a general rule, consolidate all the feedback you receive in writing. If the client sends feedback via e-mail, that makes it easy. If the feedback is given during a call, make sure to take detailed notes and then summarize the outcome of the conversation to send to the client for confirmation.

If you have doubts about the feedback, be sure to inquire. Once the next steps are clear, based on the feedback, you can tell the client what to expect from you and when.

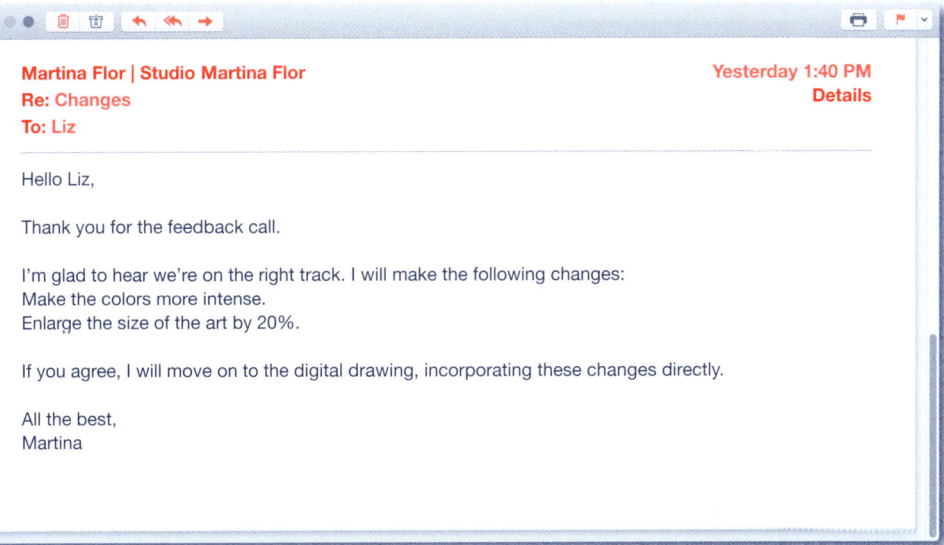

Delivering Final Files

Your project is due today! It's time to prepare the final files. Depending on your line of work, delivering a project can mean different things. The technical requirements involved in preparing final files will vary depending on the nature of the project—a digital illustrator will be dealing with different files than a photographer or a product designer, for example. In all cases, the client must receive your files ready for implementation. Getting this right the first time around will score you points and save you from having to backtrack after the job is delivered.

Before making the files available to the client, make sure that they are in the appropriate format and that they align with the specifications outlined in the brief. Document your final files on the private page you set up and then let your client know in an e-mail that the files are ready. Don't forget to provide a link!

Make sure you get confirmation that your client has downloaded the files and that everything is in order.

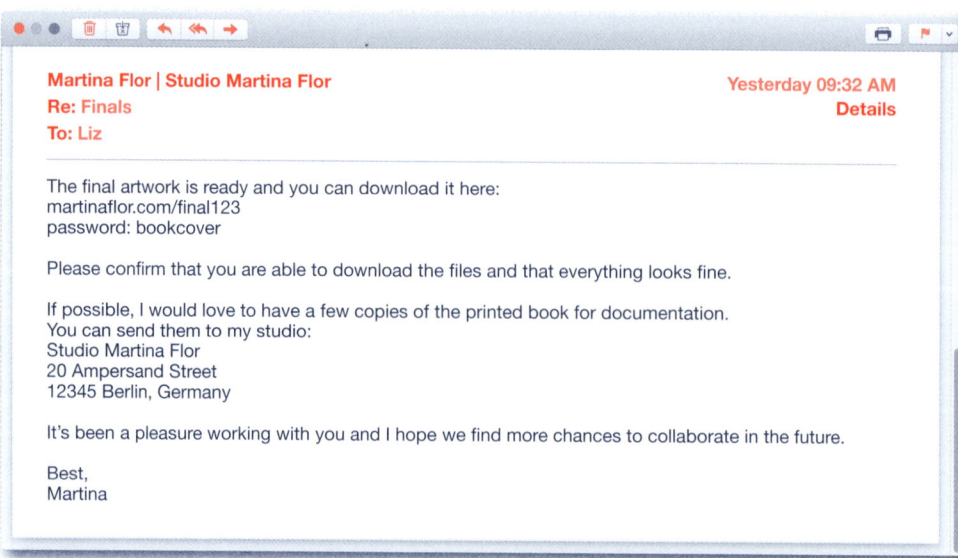

Requesting Material for Documentation

The client downloaded the files and everything is formatted correctly—congratulations! Now is the time to wrap up this commission. What comes next is purely administrative: billing.

But before saying goodbye and thanking the client for making this job a pleasant one, you might want to request physical copies of what you worked on. It's a good idea to keep a record of everything you produce, and requesting physical copies is part of this archival process. Physical copies can be showcased on your website and social media networks, and are useful tools for promoting your work and ultimately, attracting new commissions. As soon as you receive physical copies of your work, take some photographs for your website and then add them to your archive. Objects such as books and prints might come in handy in the future, if your work is being exhibited, for example, or when you need something to bring to a meeting with a new client.

Getting Paid

Sending an invoice is, as you can imagine, very gratifying. Beyond getting paid, sending an invoice means that you have, once again, succeeded in doing what you enjoy, and that you're good at it. So gratifying!

Ideally, you'll want to prepare and send your invoice within forty-eight hours of getting confirmation that your client has received and reviewed the final files. You are now truly finishing the project. Although what's on an invoice may vary from country to country, all invoices generally contain the same elements. Create invoices that have your branding (your logo, any other visual brand elements, and contact information), so the customer can easily identify who to pay.

Include the following on every invoice:

<u>Invoice number:</u> This will help keep your accounting organized and allow you to easily track your invoices.

Your business information: Your name or the name of your studio, and all your contact information—all essential for billing (and getting paid).

Account information or payment methods: Provide details of the name of the account holder (usually you), the account number, and other relevant information. If you use other payment methods or apps, such as PayPal or Venmo, include your e-mail and/or username.

Project name: Use a project title that is clear and easily recognizable.

Job details: Include a description of what you're invoicing for, whether it is a two-color illustration, or a corporate logo for letterhead.

The amount: Of course, you'll want to provide the amount you're billing for, plus taxes if applicable.

General considerations and rights of use: You can reiterate some of the points that were agreed upon when you secured the assignment. If you have agreed on a certain license period, for example, you should include that on the invoice.

Signature and date: Sign by hand or include a digital signature. Include the date so that the client has a reference for when to send the payment.

Payment terms: These terms outline the time frame within which the payment must be made. Your invoice may also stipulate a surcharge that will be added if the payment is overdue.

Confirm with your client which other information you need to attach together with your invoice. In the United States, if it's your first job for a certain company (over $400), you'll need to send a signed tax form (W-9) with your invoice (in this case you may want to encrypt the file, which is easy to do in Word, since it includes your social security number).

The person you invoice may not be the same person with whom you carried out the creative process. The client should let you know who to bill.

If you are reaching out to a new contact for the first time, remember to introduce yourself and indicate the project for which you are invoicing and the name of the person who assigned you the project.

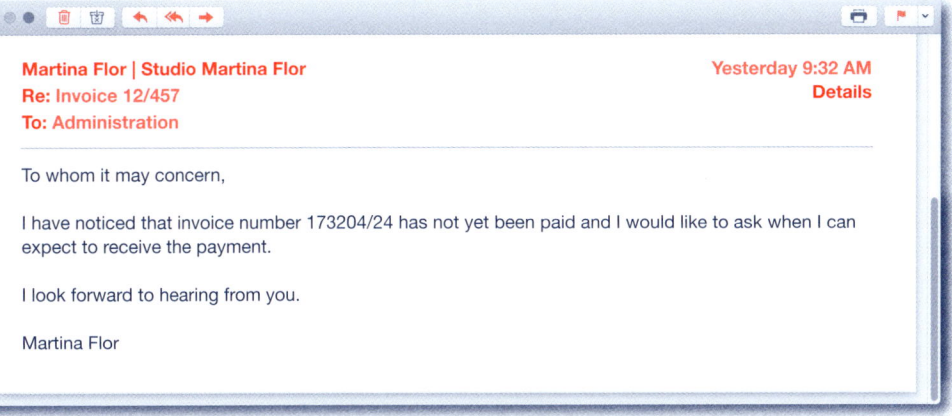

Here's a tip: add an alarm in your calendar that reminds you to check that the payment has been delivered to your account.

Getting Paid for a Job

The importance of charging for your work is obvious. However, depending on whom you're working with, where they are based, and other factors, your payments might occasionally be delayed. It's unfortunately very common for freelancers to have to write to clients to request payment for an overdue invoice.

Part of your job will be to make sure payments are made. To this end, keep track of your finances, as outlined in chapter 5, to keep abreast of which payments have come in and which are outstanding. Keep in mind that a customer's late payment might prevent you from paying your own business expenses on time, possibly causing you to incur additional costs. All the more reason to send a friendly, but firm, e-mail as soon as you discover an overdue invoice.

Organize your end-of-assignment process. Create a checklist you can follow every time you complete a project for a client. It should include sending an invoice, requesting hard copies of your work, establishing payment terms, following up on late payments, and anything else relevant to your discipline. This process can ultimately become part of your operations manual.

8. Sustainable Growth

This chapter will cover some important issues around developing a thriving and sustainable practice. We will talk about customers, values, and ourselves as living, working instruments.

Keeping the Right Distance

The key to building any sustainable career is working well. Working well is not just about achieving aesthetically pleasing results; it also involves you, the creative professional—your intelligence, adaptability, and personality. A successful freelancer knows how to interpret a briefing, incorporate feedback, and deliver work in a timely manner. The human factor plays a fundamental role: for a client to be satisfied she must have a good experience working with you on the project.

Creative work involves much more than technical knowledge. Here, your emotions and your ego play an important role. It can sometimes be difficult to maintain emotional distance and to keep a cool head when managing a project. When we send an initial proposal to a client, we do it thinking that what we're proposing is the best solution. Getting negative feedback or, worse, having your proposal plainly rejected, can be tough and frustrating. This situation has inspired countless memes about the freelancer-client relationship (most of the time involving dogs and cats fighting). We've often put a lot of work and plenty of heart into what we're doing, so our first reaction to negative feedback can be to defend ourselves.

But there is something you should always keep in mind when you do an assignment for a client: the client wants the result to be extraordinary as much as you do. The customer wants the piece to work perfectly, and you want it to be a piece worth adding to your portfolio.

"Educating" Customers

In our disciplines, we work with people who also have feelings, who have good days and bad days. It is part of your job to learn to deal with the people we have been referring to as "clients."

Not every client we work with will have the same level of experience leading assignments that involve creative specialists. In other words, not everyone will be an expert in design, illustration, photography, or copy editing. Therefore, you may need to strengthen your communication skills. If your client doesn't have typography knowledge, for example, you'll need to briefly explain why you chose the typeface you chose for the catalog you are developing; if you're a photographer, you may need to explain why it's more advisable for the subject of a portrait to look to the right instead of the left; if you're a graphic designer, you may need to explain what a vector drawing is and why it takes so much time. And you'll need to learn to communicate what you're doing so that a person unfamiliar with your professional field can understand. Learning to guide your client through all the stages of the process in a comprehensive and accessible way will give you a huge leg up over the competition and ensure that you get repeat customers.

Working in Different Markets

Dealing with international clients can reveal how standards and practices in your field vary from market to market. You might notice that briefs from clients in a given market are particularly detailed, or that the feedback you receive from clients in another market is consistently vague. In some markets, assignments might regularly extend beyond established deadlines (perhaps resulting in a greater number of headaches!).

Creative disciplines and industries have developed unevenly in the world. In some places, disciplines like ours are deeply established. These are markets that have long relied on graphic design, photography, illustration, and advertising to position and move products. In some "newer" markets, however, creative industries are just gaining traction. You may have to work harder at educating clients in such places.

Defining Standards for Your Work

When you receive a query for an assignment, take a moment to think if you really want to accept it, because once you do, you must give it your all.

Most everything you produce nowadays is stored somewhere on the internet. Your projects might be displayed in the street or available at the library. Everything you work on represents you as a professional. That's why it might be helpful to define personal standards that your work must meet.

Avoid working for clients who want quick and dirty solutions. Clients who care more about efficiency than quality, who keep you working against the clock under stressful circumstances, are bound to get unsatisfactory results. On the other hand, clients who put quality at the center of everything they do will allow you to develop ideas, make mistakes, look for solutions, learn things along the way, and arrive at more pleasing results.

You get to decide which assignments you take on—that is your great power as a freelancer. The standards you set for your own work will translate into the kinds of clients you attract, and not the other way around; if you produce high-quality work, then you will only need to accept assignments that set you up for growth and success.

You can set ethical standards for your work as well. You can decide not to do work for companies that represent causes or issues that you don't support. By contributing your work to, and taking money from, clients and companies, you are, in a sense, agreeing with what they do and stand for. Be informed about both the client as well as their intended use of the project you are going to work on. As far as quality is concerned, you can set standards that encourage you to pay attention to small details, for example, or retain a high level of technical proficiency in your drawings. These criteria will be different for everyone, and will vary across disciplines.

This is a lettering job that I accepted a few years ago without first getting all the details. When I got down to work, after signing the contract, I realized that I did not agree with some of the messages I was lettering. As creatives, our job is to help to communicate a message. Understanding what we are contributing to should be part of our decision-making process when we are offered a job. Do not contribute to anything that goes against your principles.

The standards I set for my work are as follows: (1) the text must be legible, (2) the elements must complement one another, (3) each element must be executed with care, (4) the design must respond to the requirements of the assignment, (5) the design must be beautiful, and (6) the design must be novel. Make your own list of standards that, from now on, every job you do will meet.

Retaining Clients

If you have done a good job (you have followed projects through to success, you have been pleasant and professional, you have listened to the client's feedback, and you have done your best at each stage of the process), it is very likely that the client will consider you again for future jobs and recommend you to others.

    A client who has worked with you before will probably consider you for a new project, mostly because you have become a dependable resource. You made a positive impression in everything you did: from how you managed each step of the process, presented your work, and delivered a high-quality result, to the letterhead you used to send your quote, the sizes and colors of the fonts you picked, and the brevity of your e-mails. Great! In order to retain this happy client, you will need to maintain the same standards she now expects—so it's important that your process is repeatable.

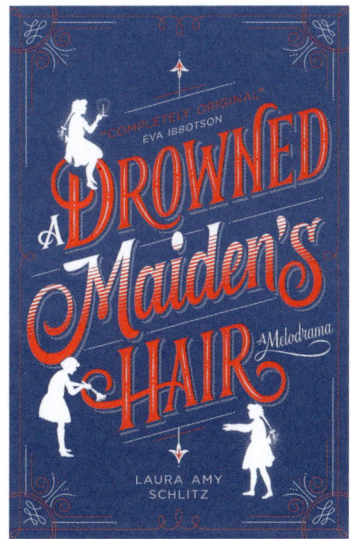

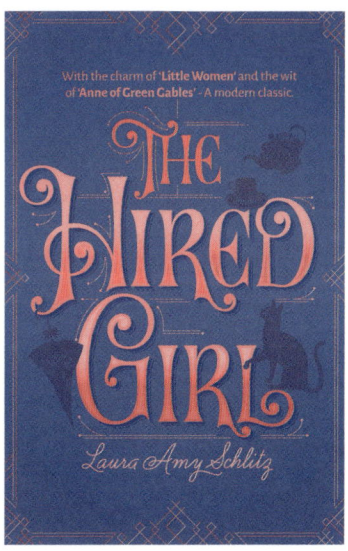

We talked earlier about the benefits of organizing our creative process and dividing it into stages. Having an organized process is also useful for retaining clients. If a client is happy with your work, you can simply repeat your process the next time they call on you.

Attracting Better Assignments

The quality of assignments you attract is directly related to how reliable you are. As you gain experience and carry out successful projects, you will become a safe bet.

Clients will know what to expect from your process and come to rely on the outstanding results you deliver. Trust commands a price and your clients are willing to pay for it.

Once you have built trust, you can start changing the way you calculate your fees—yes, you can start charging more!

Previously, we talked about two models for calculating the value of your work and putting together quotes—hourly, and on a project basis. It's easier to transition from an hourly model to charging on a project basis (see chapter 6) once you have established trust. Your project fee should cover your hourly rate and then some, accounting for your experience, and the likelihood that you will carry out the project successfully and efficiently.

While charging more for commissions is undoubtedly an improvement, it is also key to attracting larger and more lucrative commissions. Next, we'll talk about concrete actions you can take to get more challenging assignments (that pay more!).

<u>Improve your skills:</u> Take a workshop, work on side projects, and read books (like this one you now have in your hands). All the skills and knowledge you acquire will make you a better professional and give you the ability to tackle new tasks. Things change very quickly and you have to stay current. Dismissing new tools and skills (simply saying "programming is not for me," for example) undermines your chances of progressing.

You don't have to be the best at everything, but you do need to have an idea about what's going on at the forefront of your discipline, how new tools and processes work, what you can accomplish with them, and who in your professional network might be an expert in them. If a project requires a skill you haven't yet mastered, you can seek help from your network.

<u>Make proposals to your clients:</u> Instead of waiting for projects to come your way, you can volunteer to take on new work for established clients. For example, if you are hired to redesign a logo, you can put yourself forward to take on further brand identity work. If you are asked to take photos at a company's tenth anniversary celebration, you can propose a photo-report with interviews and portraits of that company's employees.

Customers tend to be enthusiastic about good ideas, especially if someone can take the idea and run with it.

<u>Rethink how you introduce yourself:</u> It's been a while since you decided to take the big leap and work on your own. You are

now someone with experience, financial security, and a good reputation. Does your profile picture on your website speak to how you'd like to position yourself right now? Your bio and your website may also need to be reviewed. The commissions you receive reflect how you show yourself to the world.

Up your game: By the time you've earned a reputation, you will probably have experiences to share and wisdom to pass on. If you're up for it, this could be a good time to up your game and try teaching and speaking. Have you been wondering what it would be like to speak at conferences? Apply for a talk. Are you passionate about teaching? Go ahead, record your first online class or organize your first workshop. Have you had to create digital tools for use on your assignments (e.g., brushes, or a collection of icons)? Monetize them by posting them for sale for others to use as well.

Diversifying your income broadens your audience and creates a multilayered business that feeds itself. A student in one of your online classes may also want to buy those vector drawing brushes you used for a demonstration in the class. A conference attendee who enjoyed your talk might follow you on Instagram or sign up for one of your upcoming online classes. You can be in a lot of places at the same time!

Taking Care of Your Most Important Tool: Yourself

You will initially be the engine of this project—the bulk of your work force—and therefore you must take your self-care seriously.

You work in a discipline you enjoy, which is great news. It's still work, though, and you still have deadlines to meet, so pressure and staying on top of your schedule is part of the deal. Because we like the work, it's easy to find ourselves going full steam ahead during all waking hours. But not taking breaks can lead to stress and discomfort. And doing too much of the work we love can eventually make us hate our work. Don't overload yourself. You may find yourself making changes well after working hours because "it'll only take a minute," and you can "just get it done." You're your own boss—don't be the most unforgiving boss you've ever had. Assign time in your schedule for meals and breaks. Set a timer to remind you to get up and walk around if your job requires you to sit for hours at a time. And of course, think twice before taking on an assignment with an impossible deadline that will require you to work through the night. Rest is essential—your brain will offer up better ideas and you will be more productive after a good, long sleep. Don't let projects dominate your life, and don't eliminate the things that you enjoy. Schedule time for things that keep you sane and make you happy.

Delegating Tasks

Part of not abusing the workforce you have—you—is knowing when to delegate tasks. Hiring help doesn't necessarily mean having employees, but it can mean occasional collaborators who free you from certain tasks and give you time to devote to thinking about the future of your business.

As your business progresses and your reputation and value as a professional increases, you will become "too expensive" to perform certain tasks. The tax return that you used to take two days to complete might need to be handed off to an assistant or accountant. Maybe it no longer makes sense for you to spend time cleaning your office, and you can hire someone to come in occasionally. In the end, handing off these kinds of tasks can turn out to be a cost-saving decision, if you spend those newly free hours looking for new clients, promoting yourself, or planning the next steps for your business.

Recruiting Help

As your business grows, it will require more and more management to thrive. The projects will be bigger, the responsibilities greater, and the consequences of mistakes or mismanagement more severe. Delegating some of your work will allow you to get rid of the day-to-day tasks, and adopt a more visionary role, one in which you get to strategize about how to get your business

It took me a long time to understand that when I take care of myself I do a better job. I used to believe that the standard of a successful frelancer was being overloaded with assignments, working after hours, and skimping on sleep. This often affected my motivation as well as my capabilities. Don't lose sight of the fact that this is your opportunity to create the perfect job situation for yourself and make yourself happy.

from where it is to where you want it to go. Those of us working in creative disciplines truly own the concept of authorship—our work carries our personal mark. It's easy to feel that if you don't do it yourself, it won't have the same personality and heart. "No one can do it like me," you might think, "and therefore, I need to do it all!"

However, you have only two hands. If you want to grow, you need to step back from the business and let some things go. Trusting others, you can accomplish more. Yes, I know that's tough to hear.

There's surely a part of your creative process that can be executed by someone else: if illustration is your thing, you don't need to scan the sketches yourself or export the PDFs of your client presentations; if you're a photographer, you probably don't need to mount and dismantle the photo set yourself every single time; if you're a typeface designer, you can delegate the letter spacing to someone else; if you have an online store, you can ask someone else to upload images of new products. There is always something that can be executed by someone else. Imagine creating the overall concept for an assignment and having someone else enter the changes requested by the client; changes like, "Move this half an inch to the right," or "Increase the image size by 20 percent," or "Add 0.1 inches to the bleed." Sounds good, doesn't it?

When it makes sense for you, your role can shift from designer to supervisor, trusting others while ensuring their work is done to your standards. Here is the most wonderful thing about delegating work: it will help you see your results with an impartial eye. You will gain critical distance, and become more capable of seeing what requires tweaking, since you will no longer be responsible for executing minute changes. It's true that hiring help can be costly, but it'll very likely result in more profit. If you're doing well and you want to scale your business, take a chance and shift your role. If actually hiring an employee seems like too much of a risk for you, start small. Take on an intern or a hire a freelancer. This experience will get you used to having help, and demonstrate that more hands do more work!

Dealing with the Competition

Perhaps many people do what you do. The good news is that nobody does it exactly like you. Due to globalization and the social media boom, we are constantly exposed to what others are doing, working on, and producing, in the same way that others are exposed to what we post and share. Looking at what everyone does all the time can be a great source of inspiration, but can, at times, make us feel unproductive and insecure about our own work: "Am I doing my best work?" "Am I ever gonna be as good as that artist?"

A photo of my second open studio event. It would not have been possible without a team, because it was a tremendous amount of work selecting from among all my work from the past ten years. This book you're reading right now is the result of teamwork: Soraya (a past intern) and designer Josefina Anglada (our project manager) produced all the photos for this book. Talented designer Elías Prado was responsible for the layout.

In today's media landscape, it is easy to become so inundated with images and influences that we lose track of what we're taking in. The key to making unique work, and to enjoying your process, is to use yourself as a reference; you need to compete only with yourself. Focus on finding ways to improve your work instead of paying attention to what others are doing. This approach will naturally differentiate you from your competition. Additionally, expand your references. Log off, and go to the library or a museum; take time to observe your surroundings on walks or in the grocery store. Look for inspiration in unexpected places. Do independent research, exploring stylistic movements from other eras and other disciplines.

Do your work in the best possible way, regardless of what others do, and track your own progress. In six months, you will look at that illustration you did today, or that portrait photo you shot, and think "I could do that much better now." You can get better at what you do by playing your own game.

What's Next

The first year as a freelancer is tough, but it probably won't be the hardest of all. When you take the big leap, you will ideally have a network of acquaintances and personal connections in place who will open doors, pass along jobs, and connect you with other creatives who can help you create even more connections. This network will hopefully provide enough initial work to keep you busy laying the foundation of your business. During your first year, you will get to see how it feels being self-employed, face your first problems, and experience your first exhilarating successes. You will learn a lot!

Keep your vision, your true north, in front of you at all times. Even if, in the beginning, you are on your own, working on your website while hoping an assignment will come through, don't lose sight of where you want to be in a few years. This will give you daily motivation.

As you move forward with your freelance career you will come up against new problems. However, you will also have better-refined tools and more resources with which to deal with them. Things that you worried a lot about in the beginning will become second nature and you'll have more time to invest in what you like doing. The ultimate goal when you take the big leap is to build a business that truly works for you—keep working, and you will!

For useful links and additional material, check out the free online resources I have prepared at: **www.martinaflor.com/ thebigleap.**

Afterword

Hopefully the material in this book has given you space to reflect and inspired you to take the big leap. If you've already started down the entrepreneurial path, perhaps this book has given you new ways to think about certain aspects of your business. It's impossible to know before you start whether you will succeed as a freelancer. Now, at least, you have tools, resources, and knowledge to help you as you embark on this adventure and give it your all.

    There's no one formula, and there are simply no guarantees. It's up to you to take a chance and see what works. On the way, you'll find joy and success, and make mistakes. You'll have fear and, at times, feel very little motivation. It's part of your new job description to keep on moving, even if at times it seems that the wind isn't blowing in your favor. Give it time, as this process won't happen overnight. You'll have to work and be patient to see positive results. You can only begin, and slowly build yourself up from there. I wish you the best of luck as you plan your first steps, and hope this book will continue to serve as a companion as you make your big leap!

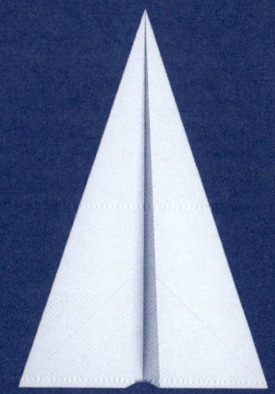

Acknowledgments

Thank you to all those with whom I have had passionate talks about freelancing and entrepreneurship: Matteo Bologna, Josefina Álvarez, Neil Summerour, and Sol Matas. And to my coach, Diego Bresler.

    Thanks always to my parents for supporting me in all the paths I took. To all my students around the world, thanks for asking questions and inspiring me to write this book. To Josefina Anglada, Soraya Cremallé Sa, and Elías Prado, thank you for being essential to this project and for helping me to shape it. Thanks to my family, Ilja, Milo, and especially Felix, who came into the world as I wrote this book.

Stay in touch: www.martinaflor.com/share

  @martinaflor

Also by Martina Flor: